# *The* Wild Horses *of* Assateague

THE HOOFPRINTS GUIDE TO

# *The* Wild Horses *of* Assateague

Written and Illustrated by
Bonnie U. Gruenberg

QUAGGA PRESS

*The Hoofprints Guide to the Wild Horses of Assateague*

ISBN 13: 978-1-941700-03-7

Library of Congress Control Number: 2015936072

Published by Quagga Press, an imprint of Synclitic Media, LLC 1646 White Oak Road • Strasburg, PA 17579 • www.quaggapress.com

Also by the author
> *The Wild Horse Dilemma: Conflicts and Controversies of the Atlantic Coast Herds* (Quagga Press, 2015)
> The Hoofprints Guide Series (Quagga Press, 2015)
>> Assateague
>> Chincoteague
>> Corolla
>> Ocracoke
>> Shackleford Banks
>> Cumberland Island
> *Hoofprints in the Sand*, Kindle Edition (Quagga Press, 2014)
> *Wild Horses of the Atlantic Coast: An Intimate Portrait*, Kindle Edition (Quagga Press, 2014)
> *Hoofprints in the Sand* (as Bonnie S. Urquhart; Eclipse, 2002)
> *Essentials of Prehospital Maternity Care* (Prentice Hall, 2005)
> *Birth Emergency Skills Training* (Birth Guru/Birth Muse, 2008)
> *The Midwife's Journal* (Birth Guru/Birth Muse, 2009)

Forthcoming
> *Wild Horse Vacations: Where To See the East Coast Herds and What Else To Do While You're Visiting* (Quagga Press, 2015)
> *Wild Horses! A Kids' Guide to the East Coast Herds* (Quagga Press, 2015)
> *Birth Emergency Skills Training*, 2nd Edition (Synclitic Press, 2015).

# Introduction

In July 2010, record high temperatures drove people to the shore, where they staked territory on the beach hoping to catch a blessed sea breeze. I was no different. As the mercury topped 100°, I joined the mighty throng of escapees to the Maryland end of Assateague Island, laid out a towel, raised an umbrella, and popped up my shelter. When I looked up to survey the landscape, the incongruity momentarily startled me. Even after decades of regular visits, the scene seemed bizarre. On Assateague, among the multitude of noisy families and the prostrate sunbathers, wild horses lay snoring in the sand, wandered among visitors, and splashed in the surf. Across the dunes, in the camping area, wild horses ransacked tents and opened coolers, looking for food. Millions of people prefer Assateague over any other beach largely because it is home to free-roaming horses that are clever, crafty, and wholly acclimated to the presence of people on the islands that they and their ancestors have roamed for hundreds of years.

More than 2 million people visit Assateague Island National Seashore every year, crowding into the developed areas or hiking out to enjoy solitude in maritime wilderness. Yet most people who spend time on this beautiful island are unfamiliar with its unique history, its environmental concerns, and the political winds that shape policies affecting it. The majority of people who visit Assateague to watch wild horses have no knowledge of their history, their behavior, or their bio logical realities.

When I first started researching the wild horses in the mid-1990s, I was surprised to find that wild horses lived on a number of Atlantic barrier islands and had once ranged along much of the Atlantic coast. They made their first hoofprints there not long after the arrival of early European -settlers, and in time they ran free on innumerable North American islands and peninsulas from the Caribbean to Canada. I learned that small herds remained on the coast of Virginia, North Carolina, Maryland, and Georgia; on Sable Island, off Nova Scotia, Canada; and on Great Abaco Island in the

Bahamas. Each population of horses has its own character, its own history, and its own set of problems. In most cases, these animals have made a unique contribution to local history, and each herd has its own detractors and defenders.

After my first book, *Hoofprints in the Sand: Wild Horses of the Atlantic Coast*, was published in 2002 by Eclipse Press, I dove in deeper, interviewing experts, evaluating the evidence, and monitoring the herds. I explored management conflicts that encompassed political, economic, and cultural issues as well as purely scientific ones. I studied storms and shipwrecks, equine be-havior and genetics, history, epidemiology, barrier-island dynamics, sea-level rise, beach devel-opment, and the perpetual clash of viewpoints. I studied hundreds of documents, from historical papers to scholarly journals to court transcripts, so that I might accurately present the pertinent issues. Distilling all this information, I tried to present all sides of the issues fairly so that readers might reach their own conclusions. The result is *The Wild Horse Dilemma: Conflicts and Controversies of the Atlantic Coast Herds* (Quagga Press, 2015) the most comprehensive work ever published about these horses.

Wild Horse Dilemma is exhaustively researched, copiously documented, and peer-reviewed; but at 600 pages it may be too long for many people eager to learn about a particular herd. For readers with limited time, I created the Hoofprints Series. Excerpted from *Wild Horse Dilemma* and containing additional photographs, each Hoofprints book presents a single Atlantic Coast herd in sufficient detail to satisfy both the layman and the academic.

I take all my wild-horse photographs though telephoto lenses that let me to keep my distance. When horses approached, I retreated. My goal has been to remain so peripheral to their lives, they will forget that I am nearby. Because countless people have stroked them, fed them, and lured them, some can be momentarily docile, occasionally indifferent, or routinely bold and pushy in the presence of people. As anyone bitten or trampled can attest, they are no less wild than horses that avoid human contact. When we impose ourselves and our desires on their lives, when we habituate them to our presence, when we teach them to approach us for food and at-tention, we rob them of their wildness. When we treat them as we would their domestic counter-parts, we miss the opportunity to observe them in a natural state, that is, to appreciate the things that make them irresistibly attractive. We miss the very point of driving past thousands of their tame kin to seek them out. We create something like a petting zoo hazardous to us and to them. If we truly love and respect wild creatures, we must learn to stand back and enjoy watching them from afar. Only then can they—and we—know the real meaning of wildness.

As the earth's dominant species, we have the power to preserve or destroy the wildlife of the world and the ecosystems in which they live. The choices we make regarding wild horses are far-reaching. We alter their destiny whether we act or choose to do nothing. We can begin to deal wisely with wild horses by understanding the facts and discovering how the threads of their existence are woven into the tapestry of life. Only through understanding can we hope to make rational, educated decisions about the welfare of these fascinating, inspiring animals.

Bonnie U. Gruenberg
Strasburg, Pennsylvania
March 1, 2015

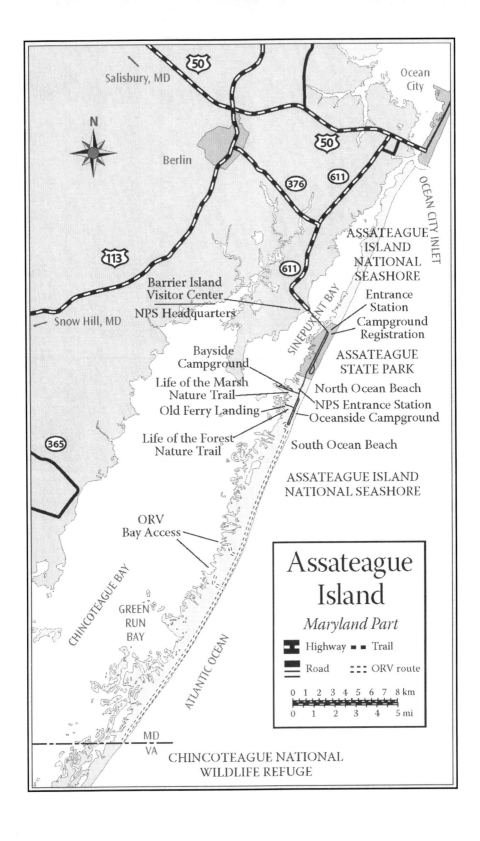

At the Maryland end of Assateague Island, visitors to the state and national parks can get quite intimate with free-roaming horses. Too intimate. The 600-lb-plus (270-kg) animals troop across campsites, block access to bathhouses, and tramp over beach towels. Bands of ponies unpredictably cross the main road, causing unsuspecting motorists to hit the brakes fast or even hit the ponies themselves. Some ponies purposely block traffic to thrust searching muzzles into open car windows, hoping for a taste of human food.

Most of the Maryland horses have little fear of people. They brazenly wander into campsites in search of good grazing and any tidbits that they can beg from obliging humans. They walk under clotheslines and step on bathing suits. They track sand across tarpaulins while families work to pitch tents. They sniff and sometimes sample food cooking inches from open fires. Itchy foals view most human contraptions, from barbecue grills to truck bumpers, as potential scratching posts. They tear large holes in screen houses and walk on in, even if there is nothing inside. Campers shoo them away with the loud clanging of a spoon against a pot. It does not frighten them, but usually signals the animals that they are not welcome and should take their activities elsewhere. On hot days, when insects became intolerable, they cross the dune line to the open beach to stand at the waterline beside the bathers.

In his book *Into the Wind*, Jay Kirkpatrick, reproductive specialist and senior scientist at the Science and Conservation Center in Billings, MT, writes about an Assateague stallion "intelligent enough to take advantage of civilization's amenities" (p. 45). Slash, a pinto stallion "with long, white slashes down his side reminiscent of seagull droppings," would avoid the biting insects by keeping to the areas of the park that employees fogged with insecticide. When he was thirsty, he would stand by a water faucet until a camper came by, whereupon he would draw attention to himself by stamping one hoof. Eventually a camper would figure out what Slash wanted and turn on the water faucet so that he could drink. "As if to thank the

While visitors enjoy a day at the beach, a band of wild horses ransacks their campsite.

camper," Kirkpatrick writes, "Slash would reward his trainee with an amazing array of facial expressions signifying his satisfaction, then drink his fill of sweet, fresh water."

Assateague is a 37-mile-long (60-km) island populated by two herds of feral horses separated by a sea-to-sound fence at the Maryland-Virginia line. Historical records document the presence of livestock on Assateague Island since the late 1600s. There are two versions of the story of their origins. For generations, local people grew up believing that the original horses swam to shore from a wrecked Spanish galleon. According to the U.S. National Park Service, they probably descended from domesticated stock owned by early settlers to the region. In colonial America, residents used grassy islands and necks as grazing commons that substituted bodies of water for fencing to contain horses, cattle, sheep, hogs, and goats. Periodically, stockmen conducted communal roundups, or "pennings," to brand, sell, or remove livestock to the mainland.

The village of Chincoteague, Va., revived Pony Penning in the 1920s after a brief hiatus, penning and selling young Assateague ponies to benefit the Chincoteague Volunteer Fire Company. When much of Assateague Island became a national seashore in 1965, most of the free-roaming horses had been moved to the Chincoteague National Wildlife Refuge at the Virginia end of the island, which allows the firefighters to keep horses there by special agreement.

On the Maryland end of Assateague, wild ponies live more or less as wildlife. Park officials interfere with their lives only to administer contraception, which limits their numbers and extends the life expectancy of the mares. Here they share a tasty morsel of *Phragmites*, exotic animals eating an exotic plant.

At the Maryland end of Assateague there remained a smaller group of native ponies. Authorities disagree on its size and growth rate. Barry Mackintosh, author of the official history of Assateague Island National Seashore, says that the Maryland herd descends from 10 horses that seasonal resident Paul Bradley donated to the Berlin, Md., Jaycees in 1965, and that the Jaycees donated the herd to the Park Service three years later. Dr. Ronald Keiper, a zoologist who has studied the horses extensively over the past 40 years, wrote that the Jayccces donated 21 horses in 1965—9 stallions and 12 mares. Zimmerman et al. (2006, p. 45) claim that there were 9 horses in 1961, "10+" in 1966, and 21 in 1967.

Eggert et al. say there were 28 horses when the Park Service acquired the herd in 1968. The team analyzed the pedigrees and DNA of the Maryland ponies and traced the current population to 39 founders with 11 maternal lineages. The number of maternal lineages in a population cannot exceed, and often is much lower than, the number of individuals. If the Assateague herd ever shrank to 9 horses or 10, it could not have preserved 11 matrilines. Either the founding herd was larger than reported, or there were undocumented introductions later.

In the 1960s, two agencies began establishing parks on the Maryland section of Assateague. The National Seashore owns most of it, but Assateague State Park occupies about 850 acres/344 ha. The horses roamed freely between federal and state property. Spencer P. Ellis, director of the Maryland Department of Forests and Parks, wanted the ponies removed, viewing them as destructive and a potential safety hazard for children. Superintendent Bertrum C. Roberts of the national seashore preferred that the Park Service acquire them as a desirable exotic species, limit their reproduction, and manage them as wildlife.

In October 1970, Roberts wrote to a colleague,

> The Service-owned herd of Assateague ponies have finally, after five heavy use seasons, become accustomed to human activity. On the surface this appears to be a great boon for the visitor. This year, however, we experienced our first cases of horse bites and kicks because of the "taming" of these wild little beasts. This according to our Solicitor must result in "do not feed, pet, or otherwise get involved with the pony" signs at the seashore entrances as well as in the appropriate park literature. It is difficult to conceive that this problem is with us at a seashore, but it is. (Mackintosh, 1982/2003, p. 105)

"All over the country, feral horses roam on federal lands managed by the National Park Service, the Fish and Wildlife Service, and the Bureau of Land Management," said Lou Hinds, former manager of the Chincoteague NWR. "The American public often cannot see the distinctions between these federal agencies, and often do not realize that each agency might have a different way of looking at the animals." One thing unites all the agencies responsible for wild horses: they prefer to eliminate them from public lands.

For most parks, management plans hinge on whether the goal is to conserve species or to preserve natural processes. If the park prioritizes conservation of species that may be compromised by wildfire, grazing, or predation, officials manage the park to protect them from these pressures. If the goal is to allow nature to take its course and accept any consequences, park managers do not interfere with those processes. If the goal is to allow natural processes to

The horses of Assateague are small, only 12–13.2 hands (48–54 in./1.22–1.37 m) at the withers. Their short stature is partly due to generations of living in harsh conditions and partly due to genetics.

occur unless they produce undesirable outcomes, park personnel intervene only when unacceptable results appear likely. Most larger national parks in the United States are managed in accordance with this third option with a strong emphasis on allowing natural processes free rein.

Two federal agencies manage the free-roaming horses of Assateague. The Park Service has total management control of the island north of the fence that runs from ocean to bay and keeps the herds mostly separate. In the past, the Park has sometimes transferred problem horses from the Maryland end of the island to join the Virginia population. Now, a wandering horse will stray around the fence occasionally, until the one of the managing agencies can return it to its home range.

The Maryland herd is managed differently from the Virginia herd. In Maryland, the Park Service owns the horses, manages them as wildlife, and has targeted a herd size of 80–100 animals. The horses north of the fence live with minimal human interference, as wild as the deer that share their habitat. The horses in the Virginia herd reproduce at will, and the foals are sold annually during the Pony Penning festival. A few of the best foals each year are "turn-backs" purchased to be donated back to the herd as breeding stock that will spend their lives on Assateague. The herd is regularly vaccinated, wormed, and given veterinary and farrier attention. In many ways it is managed similarly to Western ranch horses.

The herds have a common origin, however, they have probably been present since the 17th century, and they have become a unique and relatively homogeneous breed. These horses are pony-sized to be sure; their average height is only 12–13.2 hands (48–54 in./1.22–1.37 m) at the withers. (Judged solely by height, any horse under 14.2 hands (58 in/1.47 m) is a pony.) They are built like ponies—short legs and backs, dense bones, and thick manes and tails. There are also genetic distinctions between ponies and horses. Centuries ago, the animals were taller and built more like horses. Although it is possible that the foundation stock was mostly Spanish, outside genes have been introduced over the years. According to Keiper and others, Shetland Ponies were added to promote pinto coloration in the 1920s, and their genes might have also decreased the height of descendants. Despite outcrossing with ponies, both herds are still genetically horses, and foals sold to the mainland from Chincoteague often outgrow their island brethren.

Genetics, then, is not solely responsible for their diminutive stature. Their small size today probably results from the interplay of many influences. It is possible that tight space on Assateague limits not only their numbers, but also their size. When large animals live in small areas, particularly islands, their size often decreases over many generations in a phenomenon known as insular dwarfism. Harsh environmental conditions and low-nutrient forage also restrict growth. The horses of Sable Island, off the coast of Nova Scotia, endure a colder, stormier climate but remain larger because they have different bloodlines that predispose them to greater stature, even under adverse conditions.

Other breeds flavored the Assateague horses over the centuries, but no documented outside introductions of stock have been made to the Maryland herd since the Park Service took over its management in 1965. Until that time, there was no real difference between

The Assateague horses are in good condition overall and go about their lives with a relaxed, unwary attitude, unlike most Western mustangs. Even so, when a band lies down to rest, one horse remains standing as sentry. At the time the author took this picture, it had rained heavily for 11 straight days, and with the reappearance of sunshine, the ponies took the opportunity to nap on the drying grass.

the Virginia and Maryland bloodlines. Since then, managers have added outside horses to the Virginia herd to improve bloodlines. The current Park Service contraception program limits fertility while maintaining maximal genetic diversity in this closed population.

Assateague horses, especially those in the prime of life, remain round and robust even after a difficult winter. Carl Zimmerman, former resource manager for Assateague Island NS, attributed their apparent good health to a combination of comparatively good nutrition and the use of birth control to limit reproduction. Ponies in general tend to have efficient metabolisms and are usually "easy keepers" that stay plump on minimal forage.

From the time Assateague first became a national seashore, the horses have been free to live as wild horses, exhibiting natural behavior and subject to natural processes. Ponies may display lacerations, hoof overgrowth, or other injuries or signs of illness. Age takes its toll; elderly horses may develop prominent ribs, sharp spines, and rough coats. Because it regards the horses as wildlife,

Horses raid campsites in search of anything edible. They will also chew, unravel, shred, or crush anything else they can reach. They have flexible upper lips that can manipulate objects almost as well as fingers can.

the Park Service summons a veterinarian only if human activities have caused injury.

Many domestic horses have a far greater fear of human implements and toys than these supposedly wild ponies do. Bright umbrellas flutter in the wind, screaming children race by them to the sea, and boogie boards wash up in the surf, yet the ponies seldom shy or spook. In a camping area, inline skaters swiftly blade down the pavement, passing so close to grazing horses that they

Crossing the road often includes leaping fences.

could reach out and give them a pat. In fact, some do. Many domestic horses are at least somewhat intolerant of wheeled people whizzing by on bikes, skates, or other devices, yet these animals largely ignore the children on pedal toys that nearly collide with them at regular intervals. Dogs bark savagely at the equine interlopers visiting the campsites, but the ponies seem to know that dogs at the seashore must remain on a 6-ft/1.8-m leash—they are unimpressed with the bravado.

No matter how crowded the park may be, the horses attend to their activities unmindful of the audience. Stallions duel violently among parked vehicles and barbecue grills. Bachelor males chase one another across campsites at a mad gallop. Stallions enthusiastically mate with mares in the shade of the bath houses while bystanders pretend not to watch.

Only a small part of the Maryland section of the barrier island is tourist-friendly, and many of the horses prefer to live in the areas not frequented by people. These horses are more shy and reclusive than those that frequent the campgrounds. To the north and south beyond the camping area, Assateague is undeveloped and relatively

When horses block the outhouse, it can be difficult to use. This woman asked her husband to move the horses away so she could open the door, but he hesitated, afraid of getting kicked. Finally the horses moved of their own accord, and the woman was free to enter.

unused. Only a small percentage of visitors ever leave the developed section. Consequently, much of this well-used park remains undisturbed and natural.

Although there are many fresh water sources on the island, horses seem to prefer the cool, clean water that flows from the faucets. Groups of horses wait for campers to rinse off after visiting the beach, then take turns drinking where water collects.

Ponies and people bask on the beach at Assateague State Park on a hot July afternoon.

Park Service rangers impose fines of $175 per incident when they catch visitors feeding, petting, or approaching within 10 ft/3 m of horses or other wildlife. Many park visitors have trouble accepting that these friendly, curious animals pose any threat to them or vice versa, but they are not tame; they are just unafraid of people.

Unknowingly putting themselves in danger, tourists crowd around the horses when park personnel are absent, stroking them, braiding their manes and sharing bits of a picnic lunch. Unfortunately, this intimacy often has consequences unforeseen by many tourists: visitors are frequently kicked and bitten. The Park Service has a collection of photographs that illustrate the damage a pony can do to the human body. Often the perpetrator was docilely accepting a pat moments before the scene turned ugly.

One Park Service photograph shows a bare-midriffed child with a bright purple hoofmark centered on her abdomen. She was very lucky. A random kick can dislodge teeth, blind an eye, rupture a spleen, crush a spine or chest, or cause brain injury or death.

Offering treats can result in broken fingers when the pony bites the hand that feeds it. Some visitors offer treats from their cars and, in effect, train them to stand in the road waiting for handouts. Drivers who did not expect to see horses on the pavement hit them at speed. One such incident claimed the life of a healthy 10-year-old

The stallion defends the mares in his band from the advances of other males, but he is not necessarily the most dominant horse in the group. In most bands, the alpha mare makes the day-to-day decisions, such as where to graze and when to water.

mare. She was standing in the middle of the road hoping to stop traffic for a snack when she was stuck by a car. Her leg was shattered, she suffered internal injuries, and the car was badly damaged. Touchingly, her mate stood over her and would not leave. Park rangers humanely euthanized her.

Ticks, as tiny as pepper flecks, infest the ponies. Some of these harbor Lyme disease. Unseen, these ticks jump from pony to petter and can transmit a chronic disease that can cause debilitating fatigue, neurological damage, and muscular weakness. (The author contracted Lyme disease while following pony bands through the brush at a distance to obtain photographs for this book!) Many deer and white-footed mice on Assateague carry Lyme disease, but it is unknown how many ponies are infected. Mosquitoes can transmit encephalitis from horse to human, but only over short distances.

The Park Service prohibits visitors from approaching within 10 feet of the ponies, but a bus length is a safer distance. A horse lashing out at another will often barge right over a person standing between

A pregnant woman reviews her video footage while her toddler pets the muzzle of a wild mare. A man stands with a stroller, one hand stroking her glossy coat. These horses are unafraid of people, but they are not tame. Ponies shift gears quickly and often kick, bite, or trample people standing nearby.

them, causing bruises or broken bones. Even docile domestic horses that have been trained to inhibit aggressive impulses around people can show their irritability with teeth and hooves. Wild horses are all the more unpredictable and uninhibited.

Some visitors are downright foolhardy. One Park Service ranger told of a woman from New York who tried to ride one of the ponies. Thrown violently to the ground, she got up and remounted, only to be thrown again. When the rangers attempted to stop her, she insisted that it was okay for her to ride them because she knew what she was doing—she had horses of her own. As it turned out, she was a lawyer who should have known a thing or two about following regulations and about liability. A report in the Ocean City *Dispatch* described an incident in which two intoxicated men, one of them naked, were arrested for trying to ride the ponies and tackle sika deer.

Horses will open containers and tear apart tents to find meals. Foals learn these techniques from their herdmates at a young age. Finding caches of human food reinforces marauding behavior. Because horses knocked over trash cans and consumed everything from greasy paper towels to hot dogs, now the Park Service collects trash in horse-proof dumpsters. Rangers making the rounds

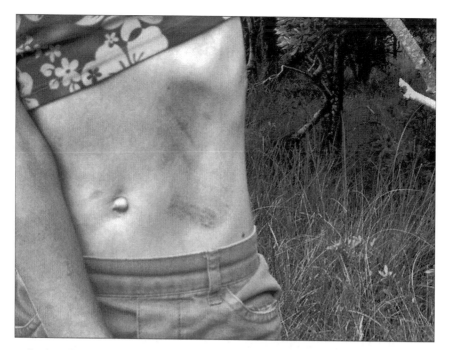

The hoofprint of a wild horse on the abdomen of a very lucky girl. This kick could have easily fractured her ribs or ruptured her spleen. Aimed slightly higher, a kick to the head or the sternum could have killed her. Photograph courtesy of the National Park Service.

of campsites will remove food left out where horses might try to get to it. Human food disrupts the balance of ponies' intestinal flora and is likely to cause colic in animals engineered as grass-eating machines. There is also little nutrition obtained from raids on human comestibles.

In the 1980s, the Park Service considered a pony a problem if it was involved in three or more documented incidents in one year that resulted in property damage or caused injury to a visitor. Before 1995, the Park Service removed a total of 39 horses from the national seashore when they became adept at raiding campsites or begging at the roadside. All those horses were moved south to the Chincoteague NWR. "Our strategy now is to place heavy emphasis on visitor education and viewing horses safely," says Allison Turner, a biological science technician at Assateague Island NS for over two decades. "By eliminating inappropriate visitor behavior around horses, 'problem horses' should no longer be created."

How accidents happen. Five drivers stopped on a narrow causeway to see the ponies and attracted them onto the road. Because other visitors have offered them treats through their windows, the horses often deliberately stop traffic and thrust their huge heads into cars looking for handouts. This horse is in an excellent position to inflict a serious bite. Note the car on the bridge, which was traveling at least 40 mph/64 kph. Its driver would not have had enough time to brake for ponies, people, or vehicles in the road.

In August 2011, however, the Park removed an 18-year-old stallion named Fabio from the island when his bold raids on campsites put visitors at risk. While most horses can be shooed away, Fabio believed that he was dominant over not only the members of his own band, but also the campers. When people tried to make him leave before he was ready, he asserted his dominance by kicking, biting, and charging, posing a significant risk to their safety. The Humane Society of the United States trailered him to the Doris Day Horse Rescue and Adoption Center in Texas, where he was to be trained and offered for adoption.

Sometimes ponies deliberately gather in the areas where people spend their time. For about a week during the summer of 2000, up to 75 ponies (which was then about half the Maryland herd) congregated in the state park day-use area, occupying a quarter-mile (400-m) stretch of beach alongside hundreds of bikini-clad bathers and screaming toddlers.

When asked why they took to the beach in such numbers, Maryland Park Ranger Rick Ward said,

Busted! The horses know the Park Service vehicles and scatter when one appears on the scene. Like naughty children caught in the act, the ponies assume an air of exaggerated nonchalance: "It wasn't me—I didn't do it!" Although the tangle of vehicles dispersed when the ranger arrived, fraternizing with wildlife cost this visitor a $175 fine.

Visitors who feed horses from their vehicles are in effect training them to stand in the road waiting for handouts. This increases the odds that cars will hit them. A car striking a horse usually hits its legs, hurling its body over the hood and through the windshield, often causing serious injury to the occupants. The car is totaled, and the horse usually suffers a terrifying and painful death. Note the bridge in the background. This automobile struck its victim directly across the road from the spot where the car was feeding ponies in the preceding image. Photograph courtesy of the National Park Service.

A band of ponies rests on the beach, where strong breezes keep biting flies from alighting.

They're wild animals. They have minds of their own. Some think they go to the water to cool off and get away from the flies, and the day-use area is just the best source of food out there. . . . they're particularly fond of potato chips. They aren't dumb—they have even learned how to open coolers!

The animals knocked over belongings, urinated on beach towels, and rolled in the sand beside sunbathers, but aside from begging food, were generally docile. The rangers concentrated on educating the visitors to avoid contact with the ponies and to keep food away from them. "Most of the time, the ponies and the visitors coexist peacefully. Very few people are a problem," Ward explained.

But he tells of one man who set out his family's lunch in a way that must have looked like a banquet to the ponies. The lifeguard warned him to put the food away, but he ignored her. One persistent pony would not take no for an answer. The man pushed and shoved at the hungry animal, then began to hit him with a shovel! After arguing with the lifeguard and lying to the ranger, the man and his family were evicted from the park.

Ward went on to relate other incidents involving clashes between park visitors and ponies:

A drunk kid jumped on the back of one on a five dollar bet and was thrown into a bush. His friends took off and left him there. Then there were the two ladies trampled by the ponies at the National Park. They were just in the way, I guess, lying on the beach. They required hospitalization.

He also told of a couple who enthusiastically photographed their toddler walking underneath a stallion, unaware that if he had moved suddenly, the little girl could have been killed.

The Park Service is responsible for the feral horses, whether they are on state or federal property, and maintains them as a "desirable feral species" (Assateague Island NS, 2006). This arrangement necessitates balancing their needs with the park's other natural resources, and keeping ponies and people safe. The park's "pony patrol" is a group of volunteers that contributes more than 1,200 hours a year educating visitors and cautioning them to stay 10 ft/ 3 m away.

The majority of visitors do not venture beyond the developed areas of the park. Their reluctance to hike into the isolated areas helps to preserve most of Assateague in its natural state. But the emphasis was not always on keeping Assateague wild.

In the 1950s, Leon Ackerman and a group of investors bought, surveyed and platted 15 miles of Assateague oceanfront property north of the Virginia line for residential and commercial lots. He advertised heavily in urban newspapers, tempting buyers to invest in his Ocean Beach development fantasies of idyllic vacation retreats and speculative profits from resale. By the early 1960s, about 3,200 investors had purchased 5,850 lots at Ocean Beach, and several dozen houses formed the nucleus of the community. Ackerman paved a road, Baltimore Boulevard, which ran to the Virginia line, and dug channels in the marshes for mosquito control. In 1957, Atlantic Ocean Estates, Inc., followed suit by subdividing the northern end of Assateague into 1,740 platted lots. The properties were promoted through radio advertisements that offered listeners "'down payments' of up to $1,000 if they could identify familiar 'mystery tunes' like 'You Are My Sunshine' and 'The Missouri Waltz'" (Mackintosh, 1982/2003, p. 14). Sales were brisk, even though there was no legal access to the property, and no streets, utilities, buildings, or other improvements ever existed.

Ocean City, Md., is a densely populated commercial vacationland with high-rise hotels, boardwalks, restaurants, amusements, and heavy traffic. If the Ash Wednesday Storm of 1962 had bypassed Assateague, it might never have become a national seashore and would probably look very much like this.

Moreover, the land in question was rapidly migrating westward—with every storm the ocean overwashed, eroding the beach and sweeping across the island to the bay. Ironically, many of the shorefront lots became quite literally Atlantic Ocean Estates as the sea claimed them. John T. Moton, the developer, was imprisoned in 1962 in an unrelated scandal.

Assateague seemed well on its way to becoming another Ocean City. In the 1930s, Assateague was surveyed as a potential site for a national seashore, but the plan never coalesced. By the early 1950s, the Park Service judged Assateague Island too developed for further consideration.

The only access to the island was by ferry, and many prospective property owners balked at buying homes in such an inaccessible location. Developers reasoned that a bridge across Sinepuxent Bay would boost sales and raise the value of the island homes, so they began construction near the ferry dock. Dredging up material from the marshes, they fashioned a causeway stub, but lack of funding forced them to discontinue the project.

Hoofprints Guide

The remains of Baltimore Boulevard, the paved road built to support the development and commercialization of Assateague Island.

Undaunted, the developers changed strategies. The state of Maryland had coveted Assateague as a potential state park, but neither its 1940 nor its 1952 proposal to acquire land there had borne fruit. In 1956, Leon Ackerman's North Ocean Beach, Inc., presented the state of Maryland with 540 prime Assateague acres (219 ha) to establish the park, fully expecting that the state would build a bridge to allow visitors and landowners easy access. The Maryland General Assembly quickly appropriated $750,000 to buy additional land for the park and authorized work on a bridge that ultimately cost the state nearly $2 million. Assateague appeared destined to become another bustling resort city—until the Ash Wednesday Storm (the Five-High Storm) of March 1962.

Although nor'easters, many of them severe, pound Assateague regularly, the Ash Wednesday Storm was powerful beyond anything in the memories of even the oldest coastal residents. This tempest wantonly destroyed almost every structure on Assateague. Sheets of seawater literally picked up houses and tossed them into the marsh. When the storm passed, the remains of 11 long-forgotten shipwrecks lay uncovered on the shore. Two new inlets sliced across the island. Twenty-two feral horses on the Virginia end of Assateague drowned in the storm. Baltimore Boulevard was severely damaged, and to this day visitors can observe large broken chunks of the roadway along the Life of the Dunes nature trail in the national seashore.

Other reminders of the storm persist. A freshwater pond stands on the Life of the Forest Trail, providing hydration for Assateague's fauna and a rich habitat for many species. The Ash Wednesday Storm created the pond when it demolished a house and whirled floodwaters around its foundation, scouring a depression in the sand to the level of the water table, where a lens of freshwater collects. The pond endures, and deep within it one can still find the remnants of the house.

After this reality check, developers and homeowners alike wondered whether the barrier island was too unstable to support a resort community. Two studies showed that for Assateague to support communities of any size, developers would need to construct a long line of large protective dunes, install an expensive sewer system, and raise the island to the minimum level recommended for permanent construction with 17 million cubic yards (13 million m³) of fill dredged from the floor of the bay. This is an astonishing amount of material. It is more than the volume of rock and soil moved to make the original 363-mile Erie Canal (roughly 10 million cubic yards/7.65 million m³) and more than the 16.5 million cubic yards/12.6 million m³ of asphalt used to pave 1,836 mi/2,955 km of Interstate 95 from Maine to Florida. Private and commercial development of the island was possible, but it would be an expensive and chancy undertaking.

Ackerman himself, having grossed about $4.5 million from Assateague real estate sales, declared Assateague unsuitable for private development. Profoundly depressed over the Ocean Beach

A study in contrasts. A wild stallion stands watch over a vast expanse of low, sandy dunes. Barely discernible on the horizon, Ocean City's geometric skyline marks the divide between the natural world and the modern one.

fiasco and throttled by financial and legal problems related to other ventures, he committed suicide in April 1964.

On the other hand, as the largest undeveloped beach between Cape Cod and Cape Hatteras, Assateague reemerged as an attractive candidate for a national seashore.

With abundant evidence that Assateague was too unstable for permanent development, one would expect lot owners to welcome federal acquisition of their property. Many, however, clung to their investments with fantasies of beach homes and profits. U.S. Representative Rogers C.B. Morton (MD 1) advocated continued residential development of Assateague. The "Morton Plan," advertised as "Assateague's reach for greatness," proposed three private villages about 10 miles apart, including a center for the fine and performing arts, sports facilities, a wildlife museum, and an auditorium. People who already owned lots on the island could trade their property for land in the new communities. When this plan drew insufficient support, Morton proposed another in 1964—a 600-acre/243-ha complex for commercial concessions and lodging. Even the Park Service initially contemplated building two

Assateague

The beauty of undeveloped seashore and an abundance of wildlife like these American oystercatchers are cherished aspects of Assateague Island 's unique nature. Yet its wild beauty was preserved almost by accident after a 1962 storm revealed it was too unstable to support development.

100-room motels with restaurants, numerous concessions, hard-surface parking for 14,000 cars, and a 32-foot-wide (9.6-m) paved highway to extend from bridge to bridge through the refuge.

A report from the U.S. Department of the Interior issued in April 1963 recommended that the federal government acquire Assateague Island as a national seashore under the Park Service while letting Assateague SP and Chincoteague NWR retain their individual identities.

The three agencies administering the island often clashed. When the seashore was authorized, the Park Service tried to assimilate the state park, which clutched its holdings tenaciously. The Park Service considered plans to increase visitation, which the refuge opposed because its primary purpose is to provide habitat for birds and other wildlife.

In 1965, the areas of the Maryland end of Assateague not owned by the state park were designated a national seashore. The three agencies agreed to minimally develop parts of the island for both intensive (concentrated) and extensive (dispersed) day use and let visitors find food, lodging, and concessions on the mainland.

Now that the seashore existed on paper, the Park Service's next task was to acquire the balance of roughly 9,000 acres/3,600 ha from about 3,500 property owners, some of whom did not want to sell. On the northern part of the island was Atlantic Ocean Estates. Although most of its 3,657 lots were owned by Thomas B. McCabe, 195 had been sold (often sight unseen) to investors. The Park Service intended to assimilate this land into the national seashore, but deemed it a lower priority, concluding that lot owners were unlikely to develop this section because there was no land access.

McCabe blocked federal acquisition of Atlantic Ocean Estates at every turn, even though many lot holders wished to sell their rapidly eroding property. By 1970, the advancing sea had swallowed much of the original real estate, and the government filed a condemnation suit for what was left. Delays ensued, many owners who had rejected government offers hoping for a better price found their holdings completely submerged by a storm in 1974.

Like all other barrier islands, Assateague is fundamentally unstable, and it has changed dramatically over the centuries. Although its coordinates, the number of inlets, and the height of its hills have changed, it has remained part of a barrier chain separating ocean from estuary with beach, marsh, overwash flats, and maritime forest. Until recently, it maintained a fairly constant volume of land mass and remained roughly the same distance from the retreating mainland.

A barrier island is the product of complex interactions of wind, waves, sediment transport, and tides, changing contour and composition in response to erosion, storms, changing sea levels, and ocean currents. Sand dunes build up, wash away, and form again in new places. Marshes are filled in, beach is redefined, and the entire island shifts westward.

In the early 1900s, Assateague was actually part of a peninsula extending through Ocean City, Maryland, and joining the mainland at Fenwick Island, Delaware. The Great Hurricane of August 23, 1933, opened Ocean City Inlet and transformed Assateague into an island again. Heavy rainfall pelted Assateague for days, engorging Sinepuxent Bay. When the winds shifted offshore and the tide ebbed, the waters of the bay surged seaward, bisecting the peninsula and forming present-day Assateague Island.

Southbound littoral currents, created by waves that hit the beach at an angle, attempted to refill the passage with sand; but by September 1933, jetties were under construction, and dredging kept the waterway open for the convenience of seagoing vessels. And because those jetties cut off the longshore currents, Assateague was starved for sand.

The Ash Wednesday storm of 1962 breached the northern part of the island in two places. Though the U.S. Army Corps of Engineers repaired them, the root cause of the difficulties remained: interruption of sediment transport, which narrowed the island and made it more vulnerable to inlet formation. Pushed by artificial erosion and accelerated shoreline migration since 1933, Assateague Island has retreated westward nearly 0.6 mi/1 km, creating changes in geography and habitat that would not have occurred otherwise.

Through the last century, engineers believed that a dynamic barrier island system could be immobilized with the right combination of interventions. Now, it is clear that "improvements" to control one aspect of the system almost always result in undesirable effects elsewhere in the system. When people build dunes and disrupt currents to hold a barrier island in place, it usually begins to lose volume. When they temporarily stabilize both position and volume, they affect the position and volume of other islands in the chain. And in the long run, nature always wins. Despite the best efforts of clever minds and expensive stabilization projects, barrier islands remain mobile and untamable.

Shoreline armoring is the single greatest threat to island beaches. Construction of seawalls and groins always leads to beach erosion over time. The Ocean City jetties disrupted the ocean currents, which dropped sand in shoals or on the north side of the inlet rather than on the northern end of Assateague. The south jetty eventually stood *in* the inlet until it was extended and reconnected to the shore using large amounts of trucked-in stone. So much sand built up along the north jetty, the Corps of Engineers had to raise the structure to keep that sand from overtopping it and filling the inlet. In 1980, the Corps recommended beach nourishment for the northern end of Assateague to combat erosion.

By this time, Ocean City was highly urbanized and wantonly sprawling northward to meet the development at the Delaware border. Engineers had supported its westward growth by filling in marshes until the Maryland Wetlands Act of 1970 limited this practice. The Clean Water Act of 1972 regulated dredging and filling activities, and the National Environmental Policy Act of 1969 required developers to conduct environmental impact assessments before beginning a project and to choose the least damaging option. In the 1980s, Ocean City widened its narrowing beaches, nourishing them with sand pumped from offshore shoals. Storms in the 1990s sucked away more of the beachfront, necessitating more sand replenishment. The ebb-tidal shoal became so large (more than 1 mi/1.6 km wide) that it merged with the northern end of Assateague. Without mitigation, the northern part of Assateague would become unstable and extremely vulnerable to inlet formation during powerful storms. Direct access to the ocean would destroy important habitat on Assateague and in nearby waters and would expose mainland communities to the full onslaught of storm-driven waves.

The Corps of Engineers and the Park Service collaborated on the North End Restoration Project to replace the sediment lost over the past 60 years to the construction of the Ocean City Inlet jetty system. The goal was to reestablish a "natural" sediment supply for northern Assateague that mimicked the way sand flowed before the jetties were built. The initial phase of the project, completed in 2002, transferred sand onto the beachfront from offshore shoals. Workers dredge the inlet twice a year to keep the channel open.

Ocean City alone hosts between 320,000 and 345,000 visitors on summer weekends, and the population of the surrounding areas has leaped prodigiously over the past 50 years. Interestingly, Ocean City has arrived at these numbers using a mathematical formula called "demoflush," which estimates population based on flow amounts through the sewage treatment system. Demoflush provides a reliable tracking method that remains consistent from season to season and year to year.

Probably as a result, water quality has plummeted in Sinepuxent and Chincoteague bays. Total phosphorus levels are 50 times the recommended threshold, ammonia and nitrogen are near the level toxic to fish, oxygen levels are suboptimal, and fecal coliform bacteria levels are elevated. If the situation worsens, water recreation and fishing may be affected, and marine life may suffer.

Some blame Assateague's free-roaming horses for the decrease in water quality. As the logic goes, each adult pony on Assateague Island produces about 40 lb/18 kg of manure each day. The 150 adult horses and their foals living on the Chincoteague NWR collectively produce more than 3 tons/2,700 kg of manure each day, and the 80–100 Maryland horses produce almost 2 additional tons (1,800 kg) daily. Water containing urine and manure rich in nitrogen, phosphorus, potassium, magnesium, calcium, zinc, and copper drains off the marshes into the ocean and bays.

This equine pollution contribution is dwarfed, however, by agricultural runoff from fertilized fields and chicken barns on the mainland and by the sewage created by 300,000 or more people, about 14 million gallons/53 million L a day. About 36% of the watershed that feeds the bays is used for farming, and large-scale chicken raising and processing are prevalent all along the Delmarva Peninsula. The highest phosphorus levels occur in June, when farmers fertilize their fields.

On the other hand, solid horse waste offers potential benefits to island plant life. Any gardener can testify that manure builds organic reserves in soil and increases its ability to absorb and hold water. It stabilizes soil against the relentless winds, assists sprouting and root

After spending the afternoon on the beach to evade biting insects, a harem band mobilizes to seek water.. In this case the stallion evidently made the decision and pushed the mares into action.

penetration of young plants, and encourages earthworms and other beneficial organisms.

Assateague is one of the most visited parks on the Eastern Seaboard, and on the island, human waste is treated in septic fields that are sometimes breached by flooding. Likewise, most of Chincoteague's wastewater is discharged into seepage pits, cesspools, and drain fields. Water quality is an issue on barrier islands that do not support wild horses as well, mostly because of wastewater treatment outfall, public boat anchorages and marinas, and runoff from the mainland.

Mussels and other bivalve shellfish are sentinel species for water quality. Because they feed by filtering water, they tend to concentrate bacteria within their tissues. If those bacteria are harmful, consumption of raw or undercooked shellfish can cause illness. The microorganism content of bay water varies widely from one hour to the next, influenced by wind, currents, precipitation, and tides. Instead of analyzing water directly, ecologists assess water quality by examining shellfish. In one study of Chincoteague and Sinepuxent bays, levels of harmful bacteria in mussels were as high as 19 times the acceptable standard for edible bivalves.

Horses appear unaffected by the increasing water pollution. A more pressing issue is finding adequate freshwater on a sandy, salty island. Seawater is about 3% saline, blood is 0.9%. When a land mammal drinks seawater, the kidneys must excrete the extra salt;

Horses have playful spirits, especially when young. Foals grow up romping with one another and teasing the older horses in the band. Like rowdy boys, adolescent stallions in a bachelor group are constantly nuzzling, nipping, and play-fighting. Through play, young horses learn essential social behaviors that determine their place in the herd, and often their future reproductive success.

but they have a very limited ability to do so. Without a source of freshwater, horses will become fatally dehydrated.

Ponies often drink the lower-salinity bay water. Assateague has small freshwater ponds, but even these have some salt content. A

Assateague

certain amount of salt is beneficial—anyone who has seen the well-worn salt licks in the stalls of domestic horses knows that the equine craving for salt is a strong one. Ponies eliminate some of this salt through sweat, some through urine.

Lost body water concentrates blood solutes and triggers thirst. Assateague horses, like other barrier island horses, may dig for water, excavating sand until they reach the water table and waiting for a shallow pool to form. Horses will often choose to dig for water rather than use freshwater ponds, even though these excavations require much more effort. The holes are generally 2.5–4 ft/0.8–1.2 m deep. On Assateague, Kirkpatrick noted that he never observed horses drinking from pools of fresh rainwater, even though they would contain virtually no salt.

A study of Przewalski's horses showed that their water intake varied from 4 L a day of icy water in winter to 20 L a day in warmer weather. Feral horses in the Namib desert in Africa may drink as much as 30 L a day, but have been known to go as long as 100 hr without water. Lactating mares with young foals drink almost twice as much water as pregnant mares. A thirsty horse can drink up to 12 L in a single guzzle, as fast as 1 L every 6 seconds.

Keiper (1985) writes that the high salt content of their water and the crystallized salt on their food prompts the Assateague horses to drink twice as much water per day as a domestic horse, every 3 hr on average. This is a sharp contrast to the mustangs of the Western deserts who may visit a watering hole every day or two.

Free-roaming horses generally live in small family groups called bands within large, overlapping home ranges. A harem band usually consists of a stallion, several unrelated mares, and their offspring from the past few years. The number of mares depends on the stallion's ability to retain them. Most bands range from four to 12 animals, but Keiper reports a band as large as 23. Band size is largest when a stallion is between the ages of 9 and 12, his prime years.

As in humans, some behavior patterns are universal throughout the species, and others vary from family to family and situationally. Many studies of horse behavior contradict each other because the horses observed in one project had different habits and preferences than those in another.

Horses communicate mostly though body language, but use vocalizations for specific purposes. Here, a stallion pauses in a parking lot to neigh to a missing mare.

The stallion remains with his mares all year and keeps them together and away from other stallions, though indiscretions occur. In the 1990s, Dr. Lisa Ludvico, now an anthropology professor at Duquesne University in Pittsburgh, determined that harem stallions sired only about half the foals in their bands!

The stallion maintains close relations with the members of his band that persist over many breeding seasons and sometimes for the duration of his adult life. Together, stallion and mares socialize their offspring, who generally disperse shortly after puberty. Most horses form tight friendships with only two or three companions, no matter how large the band.

Some stallions permit one or two subordinate stallions to remain with the band, and some bands have no stallion at all. Bachelor bands are groups formed by young males dispersed from their natal bands and older stallions displaced from their harem bands, as well as stallions of all ages who have been unable to acquire or maintain a harem.

Ranges overlap at communal sites such as watering holes. Horses claim smaller home ranges when high-quality forage, water, shade,

Saltmarsh cordgrass is the preferred food of Assateague horses, but they will consume a diverse menu of herbage in small amounts even in the presence of abundant grass, presumably to gain trace nutrients or entertain the palate. This mare forced her way into rigid, unyielding undergrowth to nibble briefly.

and other desirable features are readily available—if the needs of the horses in the band are met close to home, they do not need to go elsewhere. Because the stallion defends his mares rather than a territory, the band is free to migrate to make use of the best available resources. In resource-rich habitats, home ranges are smaller, while in harsh alpine or desert environments, they can span many miles.

Bands tend to be larger when the available forage is abundant. A number of bands that share the same geographic area is a herd. More than an aggregate of horses sharing the same space, the herd appears to be a structured social unit with an interband dominance hierarchy.

Barrier island horses graze preferentially on saltmarsh cordgrass, *Spartina alterniflora*. This fibrous and abrasive plant supplies more than half of the usual diet of Assateague ponies; American beachgrass (*Ammophila breviligulata*) provides another 20%. Island horses also consume the American three-square rush (*Scirpus americanus*), the common reed phragmites (*Phragmites australis*),

Horses can gain access to nearly any place they want to go. They enter thickets by pushing forward until branches snap. Their thick coats deflect the thorns of greenbrier. They jump fallen trees and swim flooded lowlands. They are truly made for survival.

saltmeadow cordgrass (*Spartina patens*), thorny sandburs, thistles, rose hips, and crab apples. In the winter, bayberry (*Myrica cerifera*) and elder twigs and branches become important food sources. Uncomplaining ponies munch greenbrier (*Smilax* spp.), a tough,

Birds gorge on ticks and insects plucked from the coats of horses and on invertebrates churned from the sand by their hooves.

wiry vine studded with formidable thorns, as well as poison ivy (*Toxicodendron radicans*). Sea lettuce (*Ulva* spp.) tossed onto the tideline is a special treat, rich in protein and micronutrients.

Assateague horses have also adopted an interesting mechanism for reducing the amount of sand ingested with their food, which can contribute to excessive tooth wear and induce sand colic. These resourceful ponies often knock sand from the grass by striking it against bayberry branches. Kirkpatrick writes that almost all the Assateague horses employ this strategy, but most Western mustangs do not, despite equally gritty food sources. Evidently, the animals learn the trick by copying other horses. The author, however, had a Connemara gelding who used a similar technique, banging each tuft of grass against his legs or shaking it in the air to remove the grit, indicating that a clever horse can work these things out for himself.

In July and August, when the air is still and hot, Assateague horses take to the beach, where the differential warming of land and ocean creates local winds called sea breezes. Heated by the sun, the air above the land expands and rises. Cooler air moves in from above the ocean to take its place. In the evening, the process reverses; air above the warmer surface water rises and expands, drawing air seaward from the cooler land surface.

Even when the air on the interior of the island is not moving, land and sea breezes can blow on the shore and discourage vicious insects from biting. Eventually the horses become hungry enough to venture inland to graze—to be met by an onslaught of insects that drives them back to the oceanfront. They move along briskly, distress showing plainly in their eyes as flies slice at their flanks and dozens of engorged mosquitoes pattern their underbellies like tiny red beads.

Some species of bird make a good living following the pony bands and feasting on the multitude of insects that accompany them. Brown-headed cowbirds feed at their feet. Red-winged blackbirds perch on the ponies and pluck swollen mosquitoes from their coats or pull flies from between strands of matted mane. Cattle egrets tend to feed on insects stirred up by the movements of the ponies, but they do pick a significant number of ticks, flies, and lice off the ponies themselves.

Although artificial insecticides are generally not used in national parks to control pests, Assateague State Park has sprayed for insects in the day-use area. Kirkpatrick writes that bands of ponies have been known to migrate 6–7 mi/9.7–11.3 km to gain a respite from insect attack. In 2000, budget constraints precluded spraying. Resurgent insect populations may have been why an unusually large group of horses mingled with tourists on the beach that summer. Avoiding insects takes valuable time away from feeding, but the ponies have little choice.

Biting insects are most strongly attracted to stallions and are less interested in foals. Flies—which can be larger than a quarter—feed by slicing the skin and lapping the flow of blood. A horse's skin is exquisitely sensitive to touch, and he can feel an insect land. To dislodge the intruder, he twitches a specialized "fly-shaker" muscle across his shoulders, the *panniculus carnosus*. If the fly remains, he snaps at it with his teeth, tosses his mane, stamps his feet, or swishes his tail.

Some alpha stallions allow a subordinate stallion to remain with the band. In this band, the pinto is the harem stallion, and he spends considerable energy affirming his dominance over the chestnut. In this picture, they were investigating manure left by other stallions. The chestnut then defecated on the pile, indicating "this is my home range." The pinto defecated on top of the chestnut's dung, signifying his dominance. Then they both turned to thoroughly sniff the pile again.

Bloodshed is the price of being a harem stallion. Besides being targets of innumerable bloodthirsty insects, stallions are frequently wounded in physical clashes with one another.

Mature stallions are generally intolerant of unrelated male horses. They do not lay claim to territories, but if a rival dares to invade the personal space of his band, he is obliged to defend it. On the Granite Range of Nevada, 96% of the stallions carried scars from bite wounds. Swiss researcher Claudia Feh counted battle scars on 20-year-old Camargue stallions—one carried 35, another had 146. Sometimes stallions lose their harems or even die as a result of wounds sustained in altercations with other stallions.

Although stallions are capable of vicious combat, they come to blows only as a last resort. Even fairly superficial wounds can cause lameness, infection, or death, and stallions avoid physical violence whenever possible. Bloodshed is reserved for truly important issues such as the right to mate with a mare in heat. Most of the rivalry between stallions is resolved through ritual displays.

A horse performs flehmen to investigate odors. Raising the lip exposes specialized vomeronasal organs, located in the hard palate to analyze pheromones and other scents.

A confrontation between stallions usually begins with the two participants standing well apart, watching each other intently, head raised, ears swiveled forward. Sometimes both stallions will defecate while watching each other at a distance, then move on. This seems to indicate that each accepts that the other owns the mares that accompany him.

"Stud piles" serve as a record of which stallions have recently passed. These layered manure piles are often seen along well-traveled pony trails. Stallions stop and smell them thoroughly, curl their upper lips back in a flehmen response for further olfactory investigation, pivot around or step over the piles, depositing their own manure on top, and sniff again. Flehmen is an odd-looking posture in which he stretches his neck up to full length, curls back his upper

Two stallions from the Virginia part of Assateague attempt to intimidate each other during the Chincoteague Pony Penning. Both are well-established dominant males, and neither wants to engage in a serious battle, which would probably result in injury to both.

lip, and inhales deeply. This stance allows the inhaled air to reach the vomeronasal (Jacobson's) organs, specialized olfactory devices within the hard palate that can decipher complex olfactory messages. A horse can identify the scents of the other horses that have used the pile and apparently recognize their rank in the social hierarchy. Keiper writes that stud piles on Assateague can grow more than 6 ft/1.8 m) long and 2 ft/0.6 m) high. If a bachelor herd encounters a stud pile, members will often defecate on the pile in order of rank, from lowest to highest.

If the conflict is not resolved at a distance, the stallions approach each other, posturing to determine which is dominant. After much squealing and striking the air with a fore hoof, one of the two will usually defecate, a sign of subordination. The dominant stallion will then defecate on top of his rival's manure, demonstrating higher rank by allowing his scent to prevail. Each horse sniffs at the manure pile. If the subordinate agrees that the other horse is dominant, they both retreat. Often, this alone somehow resolves the conflict.

If the issue remains unresolved, each stallion attempts to intimidate the other by appearing powerful and assertive. They approach each other with necks arched, tails high, and light, airy steps, then

The home ranges of these stallions overlap, and they encounter each other regularly. Rather than engaging in battle, they display ritual behaviors that proclaim, "I'm a tough guy, you don't want to mess with me!" Upon meeting, they sniff muzzles, necks, and flanks, their teeth and front legs facing the opponent in case bloodshed is necessary. After about 10–20 seconds of sniffing, both squeal. Another round of sniffing, another pair of ear-splitting squeals. The encounter might go on for 5–10 minutes. The one that yields is the subordinate.

jog shoulder to shoulder in an exaggerated trot known as a parallel prance. In these encounters, they appear to be sizing each other up, and if one is clearly weaker or less confident, the encounter ends as the subordinate stallion withdraws.

If the two stallions still feel equally matched, the contest intensifies. The two rivals sniff at each other, especially at the muzzle and genitals and under the tail. Loud squeals and screams punctuate these investigations. The horse with the loudest, longest squeal often wins the conflict at this point.

If not, they begin to shove each other with their weight and bite at each other, especially at the legs. The fights can quickly turn ferocious. Pulling back, they rear and strike with the forelegs—this is often a display of power rather than a means of inflicting wounds. By rearing and lunging, a stallion can knock the opponent off balance. If the conflict escalates, back-kicking and biting can inflict serious injury. When the battle is resolved, each stallion rejoins his mares and drives them away from the rival.

Stallion conflicts can last from a few minutes to the better part of an hour, the action taking place in rounds, or battles, separated by retreats to the band to graze. Eventually one of the stallions will give up and take his band elsewhere.

When a stallion grows older and slower, a younger rival usually displaces him. Sometimes the exiled stud will join a group of bachelors, but many old patriarchs become loners. A horse's drive for companionship is powerful, so this imposed isolation must be torture. Stress makes the outcast susceptible to disease and shortens his lifespan.

Experienced stallions can often bluff their way through battles with younger, stronger rivals, retaining control of a herd into old age. Keiper writes of a 21-year-old stud named Voodoo who kept a harem of seven mares and their foals despite his poor physical condition. Postmortem examination revealed that his bottom incisors had been long since worn away so that the root spaces in his gums had actually healed over.

Courtship among horses is also ritualized. Each of the pair follows a set sequence of behaviors and responses. A mare not fully in heat is unlikely to tolerate a stallion's sexual advances, so he is very careful to test her receptivity thoroughly before attempting to mate. If the stallion is too hasty and crowds a mare, she is likely to kick violently.

Ovulation is seasonal in the mare and influenced largely by length of daylight. In the northern hemisphere, the breeding season is from March through August, peaking in May and June. As spring and summer approach, days lengthen and the mare begins her heat cycles. Free-roaming horses of any given population tend to develop a breeding pattern that begins and ends more abruptly than that of domestic mares. The goal is to foal at a time when the foal is more likely to survive—after the harshness of winter subsides, but early enough in the season that the foal is well developed and fairly independent by the next cold season.

Out-of-season births have increased on Assateague Island NS from 12% in 1984 to 26% in 2001. Despite harsh weather on the island, out-of-season foals are just as likely to survive as foals born in spring.

Domestic mares are more likely to ovulate into the fall and winter because of the artificial lighting in barns. In fact, a domestic mare

While most encounters between stallions involve posturing and bluff-
ing, vicious battles do occur. This Pryor Mountain bachelor, about age
5, has been trying to acquire mares and has been repeatedly trounced
by alpha males. His coat should be glossy black; all the light marks are
healing wounds, mostly from bites.

can be persuaded to ovulate out of season by leaving the barn lights
on for 16–24 hr a day and to cease her heat periods when light expo-
sure is less than 9 hr daily.

Thoroughbred racehorse breeders manipulate heat cycles in this
way to gain a competitive edge. Thoroughbreds race against horses
with the same birth year, so it follows that horses born early in the
year tend to be larger, better developed, and faster than horses born
in late summer or fall. It is desirable for a Thoroughbred to be born
in late winter or early spring, and breeders routinely bring mares
into heat through artificial lighting to achieve an earlier foaling date.

Just before a wild mare comes into estrus, the stallion usually
attends her ardently, perhaps keeping her away from the rest of the
band or at least other males. He monitors her every move and rushes
to smell and scent-mark her manure and urine. He approaches her
with a posture that conveys sexual excitement: arched neck, high
tail, and flared nostrils. He nickers winsomely. She encourages his

Assateague

attentions by raising her tail invitingly and spreading her hind legs. A mare in heat rhythmically winks her vulva and flashes her clitoris while excreting small amounts of urine. The stallion will touch his muzzle to the puddle and perform flehmen to detect hormones in her urine.

The stallion "teases" her to determine readiness, sniffing, nuzzling, and licking her muzzle and nickering beguilingly. He licks and nibbles her shoulder, elbow, belly, and udder, then hindquarters and genitals. If she is ready for mating, the mare assumes a sawhorse-like stance for mounting with the tail deflected to expose her genitals. The actual mating takes less than a minute. After copulation, the stallion often loses interest and resumes grazing, but the stallion and mare remain close and mate frequently over the next few days.

Mares are receptive to mating for about six of every 21 days during the breeding season, but this varies from mare to mare and with the same mare from season to season. Mares can be fickle, soliciting the stallion's advances one minute and rejecting them the next. A mare will show signs of estrus before she is fully in heat, and if approached at this time, she will reject the stallion's advances with squealing, striking, kicking, and tail lashing. She is most receptive near the time of ovulation and goes out of estrus 24–48 hr after she ovulates.

The sexual instinct is present even among very young colts. Male foals test their mother's urine in the flehmen posture and ritualistically urinate over her puddle. Male foals will attempt to mount other members of the herd, climbing aboard sideways or from the front, bouncing on other males as well as fillies, adult mares, their mothers, or their older sisters. This play-acting eventually evolves into adult sexual behavior.

In contrast, fillies do not display sexual behavior until their first heat cycles. Mature Assateague mares go into heat from about March through September if they are not pregnant. They come back into heat about 7–10 days after bearing a foal. If reproduction is left entirely to nature, an average, a mare produces her first foal by age 3, and a stallion fathers foals after the age of 5 although stallions sire most of their progeny after the age of 10.

The herd accepts and indulges male foals for their first two or three years. They can get away with outrageous behavior and social

Although an average mare bears only one offspring every other year, in the absence of predators, confined herds such as those on barrier islands can increase to the point of unbalancing the environment. Note the curly coat on this foal, a trait that occasionally occurs in both Assateague herds.

blunders and most members of the herd regard them with overt affection. Colts enjoy playing with the harem stallion and may seek him out for a sparring match or mutual grooming. They impishly chew the legs and tails of adult horses, gallop disruptively through the band in a gang, break up mutual grooming sessions, and prevent adults from napping. They spend their days romping, wrestling, grazing, nursing, and sleeping. Life is good.

The colt begins to feel the effects of testosterone somewhere around his second or third spring. Mares suddenly seem very interesting. Colts are physically able to impregnate mares by the age of 2–3, but are not behaviorally mature until the age of 5–6. Keiper writes that 57% of Assateague horses leave their natal band between the 12th and 24th month. Studies of the horses of the Granite Range in Nevada showed that colts dispersed when they were just over 2 years old, with an age range of 11–52 months. This dispersal is usually voluntary; Rubenstein wrote that on Shackleford Banks, mares and stallions rarely drive off juvenile males.

Nature prepares foals for the climatic conditions into which they are born. This Assateague filly was born in July with a short, soft coat to help her shed heat. The filly below was born on Assateague in March, bearing a dense, insulated coat to protect her from winter winds and ice storms.

Since the Park Service began using immunocontraceptive vaccines to limit the fertility of free-roamng horses on Assateague Island National Seashore, only a handful of foals have been born annually. Foal mortality, however, is lower, and horses have longer lifespans, especially mares.

The heavy winter coats of this mare and foal will shed in shaggy patches as the warm weather sets in. By June, both will have sleek short coats adapted to the oppressive summer heat.

Only stallions in good condition rise to the top of the social hierarchy and acquire bands of their own. Because a harem band is dominant and has access to better forage than would a bachelor band, a colt who remains with his natal band until he is 3 or 4 is often larger, stronger, and more confident. This gives him a competitive advantage over colts dispersed at a young age. Adolescent males over the age of 2 often leave and return to the natal band at will until they eventually abandon the band permanently. Some males remain in their natal bands as subordinate stallions and inherit the mares if the harem stallion dies or is displaced.

Sometimes, stallions (or mares) will begin to harass the colt deliberately. The first approaches are not overtly aggressive. The stallion begins to punish the colt for minor infractions, biting at the legs and neck in a less-than-friendly way, like a manager motivating an employee to quit to avoid firing him. After holding an established, secure spot in the social ranking for years, suddenly he is not wanted. Most of the time, the youngster comes to understand his new status and sets out on his own.

At first, displaced colts move to the boundary between the home range of their natal band and that of a neighboring band. Neighboring stallions attack and bully the young trespassers, causing them to move on to new ranges—where the stallions of other bands chase them away.

Horses are gregarious animals and are uncomfortable without others of their own kind around. Evicted colts from the same natal band congregate with those from other groups to form bachelor bands, usually of two to four individuals but in some populations as many as 16. Bachelor bands are transitional groups that serve as surrogate family for their adolescent years.

Bachelor bands do more than provide adolescent colts with companionship. Through the frequent mock battles that make up much of their playtime, they learn the techniques necessary to defend a harem, win contests against other stallions, and establish their rank in the dominance hierarchy. They shoulder and shove one another, mutually groom, and stand with their bodies touching, taking comfort from the physical contact. Occasionally they sneak into a harem band and mate with mares in estrus.

Between the ages of four and seven, the bachelor stud reaches full maturity. If he is sufficiently assertive, he begins to steal mares from other stallions to form the nucleus of his own band or challenges harem stallions for herd ownership. Young stallions will often break

On Cumberland Island, Georgia, a stallion (right) harasses an adolescent colt, chasing him away from the watering spring, charging him, biting him, and punishing him when he investigates mares in estrus. The frightened colt responds with submissive gestures. Soon, the colt will leave the band, most likely to join a gang of bachelors in similar circumstances.

from a bachelor band and spend some time alone before acquiring a harem.

The dispersal of adolescents serves to reduce inbreeding. If young horses encounter their sires more than 18 months after leaving the band, they are treated as strangers—colts are regarded as rivals and fillies courted as potential mates. The incest rate varies from herd to herd. A study of Granite Range horses noted that about 4% of copulations were between father and daughter, though these matings are less common in other populations.

Determining paternity can be challenging. Equine geneticist Dr. E. Gus Cothran of Texas A&M University attempted to establish parentage of Pryor Mountain foals by observing matings, then confirming parentage with DNA testing, and found that his error rate was 43%. Paternity testing of 55 Assateague horses showed 36 to be sired by harem stallions, seven by subordinate males in the harem stallion's band, and nine by stallions outside the band.

Adolescent fillies leave their natal bands of their own accord, usually during a heat cycle when sexually attracted to an unfamiliar stallion. Research on the feral fillies of the Camargue region of France revealed no sign of weakening social bonds with herdmates before leaving. There was also no evidence of sexual competition between the fillies and the mature mares. In fact, the fillies refused sexual advances from the dominant stallion; and if the stallion showed persistent interest, the filly's mother would often intervene and drive him away with back-kicks.

Although some stallions retain daughters in their harems as mates, observations of wild horses in Nevada showed that stallions typically do not court adolescent fillies within their own band, even if the fillies are not their offspring. One study describes several instances of adolescent fillies who copulated with unfamiliar stallions while their fathers stood nearby, unconcerned. More commonly, the stallion will drive away the filly and her consort. When a stallion is familiar with a pubescent mare, he is not usually interested in mating with her; but if she leaves the band and returns as an adult, the stallion appears not to recognize her and courts her as fervently as he would an unrelated mare.

The dispersing filly will usually join another harem or keep company with a bachelor group. She has a choice about which band to join, inviting herself by wandering close while in heat and encouraging the interest of the harem stallion. Sometimes the stallion drives her away, sometimes he investigates the romantic possibilities. Fillies prefer a dominant stallion that can protect them from the harassment of others who wish to copulate. Often the mares in the new harem do their best to drive a new filly away. If the stallion welcomes the new addition, he will support her when the mares try to exclude her.

Sometimes a mixed group of colts and fillies from the same band will stay together. These adolescent bands are temporary, and their composition changes. Young stallions can acquire mares by claiming a newly dispersed adolescent filly, by challenging and besting a harem stallion, or by staying on the outskirts of a band until they can conquer the stallion or abscond with a number of his mares. As the colts mature, they may depart one by one to form their own bands by stealing mares from harem stallions. Eventually one bachelor is left with the adolescent fillies, allowing him to develop a band with them as his foundation mares.

Typically, young stallions are extremely attentive to newly acquired mares, nuzzling them, grooming them, and following them everywhere. They become the focus of the stallion's whole existence, often more important than even grazing.

Young mares are likely to be happy in their new herds, but older mares often have strong bonds with one another. When stolen from a harem, they may constantly attempt to escape and rejoin their mare-friends. As other mares enter the harem, the stallion will copulate with and defend all his mates, but will typically forge powerful attachments with only one or two mares.

Genetic diversity helps a population survive environmental change and disease. It also reduces the incidence of genetic abnormalities that occur transmitted by recessive genes. When a population has many unrelated individuals, a wide variety of genes combine to create each generation, and dominant genes for healthy traits balance the disease-producing recessive ones. Dominant genes for healthy traits tend to inhibit expression of recessive genes. If horses in a herd are genetically similar, a challenge such as a drought or epidemic that kills one horse is more likely to destroy the whole herd. Genetic diversity improves the chances that a population will survive by increasing the number of different responses to stressors such as drought or epidemic. Maintaining genetic diversity is a serious challenge in small, isolated populations such as the Assateague horses.

DNA analysis shows that there are 11 maternal lineages in the Maryland herd. In 2006, the population retained 95.8% of the genetic diversity of the foundation horses. Twenty-one horses out of a herd of 144 showed signs of inbreeding. Fifty years from now, the herd is expected to possess 86% of the diversity of its forebears.

If the Maryland herd can be considered a unique population, there is a balance to strike: inbreeding makes the herd more uniform but decreases disease resistance and increases birth defects, many of them lethal. As Cothran points out, "if you pass a certain point with inbreeding extinction becomes likely." On the other hand, outcrossing—introducing a horse from another strain or breed—reduces susceptibility to disease and birth defects, but increases variability among herd members in color, conformation, size, and other characteristics. Inbreeding improves conformation at the expense of health and resilience. Outcrossing improves the health of the population at the expense of uniformity. Fortunately, variability can be restored by adding an outside horse or two per generation.

Some horse breeds, such as the Lipizzan and the Friesian, have a small gene pool with no influx from outside breeds. Without outcrossing, over time, the risk of genetic disorders will increase. The American Paint Horse Association, on the other hand, encourages gene flow by accepting horses that have a Thoroughbred or Quarter Horse parent, as long as the other parent is a registered Paint. As a result, any Lipizzan or Friesian looks similar to any other, but Paints can vary widely in body shape and coloring.

How many horses are required to ensure optimal genetic diversity while keeping the herd true to its original character? How many horses can the Maryland section of Assateague support without degrading the environment? Keiper and others researched the horses and their habitat extensively through the 1970s and 1980s to determine the maximum number of ponies that the island could comfortably support. They suggested that a herd of 130–150 horses would maintain a healthy balance with available forage and native wildlife. When they collected their initial data in 1979, only 60 horses lived on the Maryland section of the island. By 1994, they had multiplied to 165. In December 2000, the herd census was 175.

At first glance, feral horses do not appear to be fast breeders. Mares can foal every year, but are less likely to produce one foal while nursing another; lactating mares tend to foal every other year. In humans, lactation inhibits ovulation and thereby conception, but mares often conceive at postpartum estrus 7–10 days after foaling. For the next 11 months, a pregnant lactating mare must nourish her unborn offspring while producing large amounts of milk. If she is stressed by disease, poor nutrition, or a cold, wet winter, she may abort the developing fetus. "She has invested less in that fetus than she has in the foal, so she aborts the fetus," says Keiper.

In many wild horse herds, foal mortality typically is about 20–25% in the first year of life. On Assateague, foal mortality is so much lower than in the West and on many of the other barrier islands, that it might predispose this herd to to rapid increases in population out of proportion to the available forage.

The U.S. Bureau of Land Management maintains that herds of Western mustangs "grow at an average rate of 20 percent a year and can double in size every four years" (USBLM, 2012, October

2). Free-roaming horse populations *can* grow by 20% annually, but these rapid increases are very short-term, and they usually occur in herds recovering from a period of high mortality or in those taking advantage of improved conditions, such as the end of a drought. Between 1974 and 1994, however, the Assateague population grew by only 7% annually, even after nearly 4 dozen horses were transferred to the Virginia herd. If the population had doubled every 4 years from 1965 to 1994, the original 21 ponies would have produced a herd of more than 3,000.

Wild horse populations fluctuate in response to births, deaths, and dispersal and typically increase when resources are abundant and competition is low. Assateague horses are also long-lived and have no predators. Disease, injury, age, and adverse environmental conditions claim some lives every year; but with annual losses of only about 5%, the death rate does not come close to balancing the birth rate.

Computer modeling predicted that, left to its own devices, the Assateague herd could swell to as many as 280 horses before starvation would begin to kill them off and limit fertility. Once the population reached 100 horses in the mid-1980s, the Park Service was convinced that the horses were having a detrimental impact on Assateague, and if they were allowed to reach their population maximum, the environment would suffer catastrophic damage.

Numerous studies convinced the Park Service that the intensive grazing and browsing of the ponies reduced plant diversity and cover, altered the balance of vegetation on the island, and threatened rare plant species. Ponies, they said, overgrazed the marsh, disrupting habitat for birds and reducing the buildup of detritus— material broken down by bacteria and fungi and eventually consumed by minute marine organisms.

When species evolve together, they produce a balanced, healthy ecosystem. Egrets and snow geese have been in a relationship with Assateague for thousands of years, as have the saltmarsh cordgrass, goldenrod (*Solidago sempervirens*), and mosquitoes. The Park Service points out that the association horses have with the Assateague ecosystem has been in place for no more than 400–500 years. As exotics, they are more likely to disrupt the balance by overgrazing, disturbing soil, trampling vegetation, and displacing native wildlife,

Studies have shown that band stability varies from herd to herd. On Assateague, above, horses tend to stay in the same harems for most of their lives. On Shackleford Banks, below, it appears that mares change bands frequently. Both groups are vaccinated with PZP to prevent pregnancy.

especially when their population expands beyond the carrying capacity of the island.

It can be difficult for nonspecialists to evaluate plausible-sounding information from experts. While conclusions drawn from peer-reviewed research are usually reliable, hard facts are sometimes woven together with speculation, opinion, or propaganda, even in official reports and studies.

For instance, Park Service officials claimed that the expanding pony population was a direct threat to the endangered seabeach amaranth (*Amaranthus pumilus*). This is an annual plant that prefers to grow on wide, naturally functioning barrier island beaches as a fugitive species, thriving or not in response to the changing island landscape. Its preferred habitats are the upper beach, sparsely vegetated overwash fans, and interdune areas. Plant counts fluctuate dramatically from one year to the next as natural forces destroy and re-create habitat. The Park service began active conservation efforts when the species became rare on Atlantic barrier islands, contracting to only about one third of its historic range. Amaranth was first discovered at Assateague Island National Seashore in 1967, but it subsequently disappeared, probably because of Park Service dune construction and stabilization projects in 1973. At that time, the horse population totaled fewer than 50 animals. In 1998, for the first time in 30 years, two seabeach amaranth plants reestablished themselves on Assateague even though the herd was near its peak census at 171 horses. The Park Service removed one plant to a greenhouse, where it reproduced bountifully, while the wild plant was destroyed by Hurricane Bonnie.

Park managers returned the propagated amaranth to the wild, placed cages around individual plants to protect against foraging horses and deer, and marked them with signs in the over-sand-vehicle zone. By 2006, efforts at restoring the species brought the total wild plants to more than 1,500 despite a horse census of 158 in 2005. Still the Park Service holds that horses are the greatest threat to seabeach amaranth, and when the horse population tops 100, the plant declines sharply.

Elsewhere, free-roaming horses do not seem to threaten the plant. On the Virginia end of Assateague, where horse range is limited to fenced parcels, the plant has "fluctuated without

Wild ponies are a unique part of the character of Assateague Island National Seashore. People from all over the world visit the park to enjoy the sight of horses against the backdrop of relatively pristine beach.

apparent trend" (Center for Biological Diversity, n.d.). Shackleford Banks, North Carolina, is home to both free-roaming horses and seabeach amaranth. The Park Service sows seed and counts plants every year, and some years the plants are more abundant than others, depending on seed dispersal and environmental conditions. Dr. Sue Stuska, wildlife biologist at Cape Lookout NS, says that she has never seen any evidence that the horses disturb the seabeach amaranth on Shackleford Banks.

Artificial dunes and beach erosion, however, destroy habitat for seabeach amaranth, and dune-building projects have repeatedly reshaped Assateague. When artificial dunes block overwash, other plants colonize the sparsely vegetated areas and ultimately outcompete amaranth. The plant is entirely absent from the stretch of North Carolina coast where the Park Service, Civilian Conservation Corps, and Works Projects Administration built a continuous barrier dune from the 1930s to 1950s; yet it thrives on the undeveloped, natural beaches of Core Banks.

The piping plover (*Charadrius melodus*) is another threatened species that thrives on undeveloped, unrestrained barrier islands.

Piping plovers are sand-colored on top and white below and are similar in appearance to their larger cousin the killdeer, with a dapper black necklace and a distinctive black stripe that runs across the head from eye to eye. The U.S. Shorebird Conservation Plan listed piping plovers as threatened in 1986, and highly at risk on a global scale. Habitat management for seabeach amaranth benefits the piping plovers and vice versa. In recent years this sparrow-sized shorebird has increased its numbers on Assateague.

Piping plovers nest in small depressions on sparsely vegetated stretches of sand, gravel, or cobble. They lay a clutch of about four eggs that resemble rocks, well camouflaged in the bare scrape of a nest. For 25–29 days, parents take turns incubating the eggs; then they share brood-raising responsibilities. Chicks are precocial—they run after their parents and forage for themselves within hours of birth, feeding on invertebrates and insects in the sand and sometimes covering more than a half mile (0.8 km) in their first day of life. During the first week after hatching, they stay warm by brooding under their parents' wings. Within 23–35+ days, the chicks can fly.

Piping plovers benefit from storm damage. They forage on sand and mud flats. They nest on overwash fans and interdune areas disturbed by storm surge. The severe storms of the 1990s wreaked havoc with many aspects of the island habitat, but they were a boon to the piping plovers, which enjoyed great productivity and increased when the storms sculpted Assateague more to their liking.

Piping plovers face many threats to reproduction. Birds, mammals, and crabs prey on eggs and chicks. Overwash may sweep away some nests, while deer, horses, hikers, and off-road vehicles can crush them. Beach renourishment programs and artificial-dune construction temporarily increase the size of piping plover nesting areas, but over the long term, these interventions cause erosion and habitat loss.

It would appear that the presence of island horses has little effect on the piping plover population. Breeding pairs on the Maryland portion of Assateague have increased from 14 in 1990 (horse census about 130) to 66 in 2006 (horse census greater than 140). The majority of these birds nest on the northern end of Assateague where storm overwash has created optimal breeding habitat.

In the interests of a healthier ecosystem, the Park Service officially manages the flora and fauna of our national parks to increase biological diversity of habitat, not carrying capacity. Clearly, horse grazing changes the ecosystem of the marsh—but these changes are not necessarily undesirable. In fact, credible studies show that light to moderate grazing *increases* total diversity of species.

How many horses are enough? How many are too many? The current population target is 80–100 animals on the Maryland end of Assateague. The Park Service allows every mare to have a single foal, then contracepts her for the rest of her life. Occasionally mares do not respond to contraception and continue to foal regularly.

On Shackleford Banks, N.C., one study found horse grazing detrimental to nesting gulls and terns, but strongly beneficial to birds that prey on small invertebrates such as xanthid crabs. Ungrazed marshes had a higher overall bird count, but grazed marshes showed greatly increased avian diversity.

Horses were a prominent native species on this continent for tens of millions of years, and it is quite possible that human activity set the stage for their extinction roughly 8,000–10,000 years ago. There is strong paleontological evidence that before humans arrived, wherever horses had access to salt marshes, they foraged on the same vegetation that they consume today. As a result, these ancient marshes may have functioned more like modern marshes grazed by horses than like those that are not. Science has not yet found evidence that ancient horses foraged on barrier islands, probably because the Pleistocene coastline is now the continental shelf. Modern horses, however, will voluntarily venture to islands if they are an easy swim from their home range, and it is likely that prehistoric horses did the same. Free-roaming horses on Shackleford Banks routinely access smaller islands in Core Sound, and ponies sometimes swim from Assateague to forage on Chincoteague of their own accord.

It may be that if Paleo-Indians reduced or eliminated the native herds of horses, they fundamentally changed the nature of the salt-marsh ecosystem into that found by early European explorers. Which should be considered natural—the ungrazed marsh that followed the arrival of humans thousands of years ago or the grazed marsh that existed for millions of years before that? Which natural state should set the standard for the Park Service?

On the other hand, because there is no evidence that horses are native to *barrier island* environments, one could argue that they did not evolve with those unique ecosystems, even though estuarine wetlands are native habitat. And whether or not they can be considered native wildlife in island salt marshes, when the number of horses exceeds the threshold the habitat can comfortably support, the environment will suffer damage.

Scholarly journals and popular media alike have published countless articles concerning wild horses on public lands. Many have accused these animals, with and without reason, of disrupting ecosystems and degrading habitat. Both sides of the argument are often heavily biased, emotionally charged, and distorted by hearsay.

The Park Service maintains that wild horses interfere with the formation and stability of sand dunes by eating dune-building plants such as American beachgrass (*Ammophila breviligulata*). Some research indicates that when horses degrade dunes, overwash increases and island migration accelerates, upsetting the balance of species living on the island. In recent years, horses have convened in larger numbers on the sensitive northern end of Assateague, and the Park Service has become increasingly concerned that they are causing damage to a vulnerable ecosystem.

To determine the carrying capacity of the island, researchers surveyed the quantity of vegetation on Assateague in 1978–1979 by evaluating the types and amount of plant life growing in a series of east-west transects. Results indicated that the ponies consumed about 1% of available foliage. Another study quantified pony forage consumption by calculating the amount of forage taken in one bite, the number of bites taken over one hour, and multiplying this by the

The natural shorefront of Assateague consists of low, rolling dunes that readily overwash. Whenever people cease to bulldoze artificial dunes into place, this natural process resumes. Wild horses at healthy population densities have little impact on natural dunescapes, but can cause damage to artificial dunes. These fence posts once held wire that kept the ponies off the dunes.

number of hours of daily grazing. The researchers used this figure to calculate forage consumption per pony, per day and per year.

These scientists calculated the carrying capacity of Assateague Island NS at 1,500 ponies. In other words, if ponies were allowed to eat every wisp of forage on Assateague without competition from any other herbivores, their numbers could rise to about 1,500 before they ran out of food. At this population density, the island ecosystem would become disastrously deranged. Most species of edible plants would disappear from the island, and non-edible vegetation would fill the void. Populations of birds, fish, invertebrates, other mammals, and even the microbial community would also suffer catastrophic imbalance. The ponies themselves would become thin, malnourished, subfertile, and parasite-ridden before their numbers began to fall. Keiper suggested that the pony population could remain in harmony with its environment if the herd were maintained at no greater than 1/10 of the carrying capacity of the island, or 150 ponies.

In 1977–1978 researchers created exclosures and weighed grazed and ungrazed vegetation samples. Results indicated that at the time ponies had little effect on saltmarsh plants, but significantly reduced the amount of vegetation growing on dunes.

Another Assateague study paired plots of land bearing artificial dunes, grazed and horse-excluded, which were selected to be as similar as possible in contour and vegetative cover. A photograph taken 7 years later shows a vegetated artificial dune surrounded by horse-exclusion fencing atop a stark, bare overwash flat. The protected area held the only surviving dune in the vicinity, the rest had been grazed bare and washed away in storms. The evidence seems to speak for itself, until we consider that artificial dunes are a landscape feature that is as foreign to the original island as are paved roads and bathhouses.

Contrary to public perception, a long, high, dune barricade paralleling the shorefront is *not* a natural feature of a barrier island. In nature, some areas of island beach receive surplus sand and build higher dunes while others develop low dunes and overwash flats. Influences such as the direction of the prevailing winds and mechanisms of sand supply and transport determine the locations and heights of dunes. On most of Assateague, low dunes and flat overwash passes are the norm. And on most of Assateague, the Park Service is allowing the natural profile of the island to reassert itself. One could argue that a healthy population of horses poses minimal threat to this more natural landscape.

Nobody knows for sure how barrier islands were created, but the prevailing hypothesis is that they originated on the mainland during a sea-level nadir. When sea level rose, high dunes along the coast apparently became separated from the mainland, forming the nucleus of the chain, which became more substantial over time. As sea level continued to rise, waves, storms, wind, and tides redistributed shorefront sediments and pushed the barrier islands toward the receding mainland by eroding the shore, overwashing a blanket of sand, and building the marsh on the opposite side.

Sea level has repeatedly retreated during the ice ages, when the glaciers were at their peak, and advanced during interglacial periods, when the glaciers melted. Since the last Ice Age, about 18,000 years ago, sea level has been continually rising, at first rapidly, then

A bulldozed wall of sand stands between the campground and the beach at Assateague State Park.

more slowly beginning about 3,000 years ago—and recently, rapidly again.

Within this long-term trend there are short-term variations. The tideline fluctuates sporadically in response to strong winds and daily in response to the pull of the moon. Ocean water directly opposite the moon collects in a mound, and on the opposite side of the globe, a similar bulge forms because of the reduced lunar gravity and the rotational force of the planet. The two bulges are high tides, and the troughs between them are low tides. The times change from one day to the next because the moon's orbit is 50 min longer than our 24-hr day. The highest tides, "spring tides," correspond with a full or new moon; the lowest tides occur when the moon is in its first and last quarters. On Assateague, the mean difference between the high and low lunar tides is about 5 ft/1.5 m.

Overwash occurs normally when storms and lunar tides push water up onto the beach and through gaps in the dunes. Sea creatures caught in the flow are doomed to certain death as the water retreats or sinks into the sand. Plant life intolerant of salt establishes itself safely away from the ocean, but overwash often kills it. If overwash reaches clear across the island, it dumps a load of sand in the marsh, killing vegetation.

This destruction is temporary, and grasses quickly root in or push through the new sediments. In this way, the western shore of Assateague gains 0.53 ft/16 cm a year. When overwash is excessive, vegetation decreases and landward migration accelerates.

Over the long term, the island naturally rolls over itself and migrates slowly to the west. Stumps of cedar forests, clumps of peat, and Indian artifacts are often seen on the beach after a storm; all these were once found on the bayside.

Storms carve inlets through the island, and ocean currents refill them with sand. Eleven navigable inlets and numerous smaller ones have been noted along the length of Assateague just in the short time since Europeans first settled the area. Communities of flora and fauna have evolved to cope with the relentless challenges of the barrier island environment.

In order to build "permanent" structures on low, unstable, over-wash-prone islands like Assateague, developers erected artificial foredunes—substantial sand bulwarks—to arrest island movement and protect roads and buildings from flooding and other damage. The state of Maryland, working with the Army Corps of Engineers and the Park Service constructed artificial dunes along the shoreline of Assateague during the 1950s and 1960s. The artificial dunes were effective at preventing the natural process of overwash for decades until powerful storms in 1991, 1992, and 1998 finally overwhelmed them.

Contractors manufacture, repair, and replenish artificial dunes through a three-step process. First, workers obtain large quantities of sand though offshore dredging and other sources, then pile it into dunes with bulldozers. Sometimes bulldozer operations scrape sand from the beach. Workers plant the resulting sand wall with rows of American beachgrass and panic grass, which grow deep roots and tall leaves that catch and stabilize blowing sand. Fences exclude the horses, deer, and people that would damage the grass and weaken the dune. The fences also catch and hold sand, augmenting dune growth.

The wall-like artificial dunes differ in shape and function from dunes naturally shaped by wind, sea, and sand. Natural island dune systems are a labyrinth of sand hills, hollows, and channels called *overwash passes*. The roots of naturally colonizing plants support

The high dunes on Currituck Banks, North Carolina, remain despite hundreds of years of grazing. Wild horses roamed the Outer Banks by the thousands as recently as the 1920s, yet the dunes remain intact. Note the irregular contours and the channels where overwash flows through during storms. Natural dunes function not as a wall to block waves, but as a cushion to absorb their energy.

and fortify the dune. Electrical bonds called van der Waals forces increase cohesion by bonding the uniform-sized grains of sand with the water between them. Natural dune systems are resilient and generally remain intact through centuries of wind, storm, and grazing pressures, even though they may migrate significant distances. In natural circumstances, dunes, beach, and offshore sand supply sustain a primordial rhythm.

On encountering a natural dune line, high water meets resistance, but can continue to overwash portions of the island. Sand is dropped in the overwash passes and builds the island higher. When the island is pummeled by storm waves, a small bluff or scarp forms, which partially deflects further waves.

Natural dunes typically change shape as they age. Flats are recently overwashed areas without foredunes where new vegetation is just beginning to take hold. As plants claim the flats, they catch sand, and the dune grows into a rounded knoll, or "embryo" dune. At the ridge stage, vegetation becomes well established. The

A band of Assateague horses rests on the dunes. Note the difference in stability evident between the natural dune, under the horse at the far right, and the smooth, easily eroded bulldozed dune to the left. In a storm, the natural dune is likelier to hold fast, and the artificial dune will probably erode.

deep and branching root systems create a dynamic scaffolding that holds the sand in place, allowing the dune to reach greater heights. Buttes are the oldest of the dunes and are probably the remnants of old ridges that have been sculpted and steepened by erosion and storms.

Overwash is essential to keeping the island in balance with natural forces. Barrier islands in harmony with sea and storm migrate westward in sync with the rising sea level. To build and brace artificial dunes is to ignore barrier island dynamics. Yet when people decided to build roads and buildings on barrier islands, the natural progression of beach migration and dune attrition became a "problem," and the response was to attempt to arrest the natural process and eliminate livestock that could hinder stabilization.

When people first attempted to immobilize dynamic islands, unnatural sand movement patterns developed. Rather than stopping erosion on Assateague, man-made dunes actually accelerated it. Artificial sand walls created a barricade that stood fast against storm waves, preventing overwash and causing erosion as the deflected water ran off the beach. Without overwash, the beach

Just north of Hatteras, N.C., overwash breaches artificial dunes with most major storms, blocking the roads with sand until bulldozers can clear it. In 2003, Hurricane Isabel, a Category 2, created two new inlets on Hatteras Island, including one 500 yards (457 m) wide at this spot. The U.S. Army Corps of Engineers and the N.C. Department of Transportation filled the inlet and rebuilt the highway. Hurricane Irene, a Category 1, also created two new inlets in 2011, necessitating restoration of the island and costing $12 million in highway repair.

became narrow and sand-deprived. The natural balance of vegetation was skewed, and sand was unable to cross the island to continue the natural migration process.

The foredunes are but one small feature of the shoreface and do very little to hold the shoreline in place. With or without the incursion of horses, bulldozed sand dikes are inherently weaker than natural dunes. They are composed of grains that differ greatly in size and shape, so van der Waals forces are less able to stabilize the sand. Bulldozing sand is detrimental to beaches. It kills mole crabs, coquina clams, and the beach microbiota, disrupting the food chain. Often the blades scrape deeper than the legal 1-ft/30-cm limit.

Studies that evaluate the effect of horses on dunes do not distinguish between natural and artificial systems. Horse grazing accelerates the disintegration of *artificial* dunes. Put another way, horse-grazed artificial dunes revert more quickly to their natural flat state.

Naturally forming dunes, such as those near the Life of the Dunes trail, endure even when grazed by horses. And in North Carolina,

Exotic sika deer ruminate peacefully by the Bayside Drive. Some wear radio collars fitted by graduate student Sonja Christensen to study habitat use (Diefenbach & Christensen, 2009).

natural dunes tower more than 35 ft/11 m at the west end of Shackleford Banks, where horses have roamed free for centuries. Horses are not allowed on the beach area or hook at Toms Cove, yet that section of Assateague is rapidly overwashing and migrating southwest. On Pea, Hatteras, and Ocracoke islands, N.C., where free-roaming horses have been absent for decades, barren artificial dunes persistently crawl across the highway with every storm and resist rebuilding efforts with a gap-toothed sneer. Great tongues of seawater flow through the breaches and rip inlets with the force of their outflow. Over the long term, artificial dunes cannot halt island migration or beach erosion—with or without horses.

The Park Service and the Fish and Wildlife Service are now trying to work with nature on Assateague rather than restricting its action. On the Maryland end, the Park Service has allowed the high artificial dune to break down, permitting nature to take its course. On the south end of Assateague Island in Virginia, natural island migration has claimed much of the beach parking area. "Land managers must spend taxpayers' money appropriately and shouldn't waste it fighting change," said Lou Hinds (personal communication, May 21, 2010). "Beach re-nourishment is not

Sika deer (*Cervus nippon*) are abundant on Assateague Island. They also range on the Eastern Shore of Maryland throughout Dorchester, Wicomico and Somerset counties. Annual hunts limit the population to about 10,000 animals.

sustainable, and therefore is not responsible. Big storms will wash all that sand back into the ocean."

While the Park Service has abandoned artificial dunes, Assateague SP has gone on building them. According to the *Assateague State Park Land Unit Plan* (Maryland Department of Natural Resources, 2005, p. 24):

> Perhaps the most important capital improvement on Assateague Island is the replenished foredune that stretches the length of the State Park shoreline and beyond, which, among its many benefits, serves to protect the capital improvements behind it from flooding and other damage. . . .
> The barrier dunes are perennially subjected to climatic and geologic forces and are in periodic need of upkeep and repair.

In August 2001 the state park began a major dune replenishment project, pumping sand from the ocean to create 14-ft/4.3-m dunes fenced at the bottom to exclude horses and people. In May 2003, an emergency dune-restoration project transported and distributed 13,200 cubic yards/10,100 m$^3$ of sand to the park's dune system at a total cost of about $256,515. After that, the agency planted beach-grass and installed a fence at a cost of $139,404. As of 2005, annual maintenance of the artificial dune involved the addition of 95,000 cubic yards/72,600 m$^3$ of sand at a cost of $717,655.

Horses are held responsible for damaging Assateague's dunes; but in truth, much of the so-called dune damage is simply evidence of a barrier island's true nature. From another perspective, the artificial dunes themselves damage the island by taking it farther from a natural state.

Horses are not the only herbivores to cause environmental damage. Two species of deer inhabit the island, the native white-tailed deer (*Odocoileus virginianus*) and the exotic sika \'sē-kə\ (*Cervus nippon*), actually a small Asian elk. In the early 1900s, Clemment Henry of Cambridge, Md., kept a small herd of sika deer, which he released nearby on James Island, in Chesapeake Bay, in 1916. Another free-roaming herd was released elsewhere in Dorchester County, Md. Later, Dr. Charles Law of Berlin, Md., purchased seven of these deer, many of which apparently had been obtained by Boy Scouts for a petting zoo at Ocean City. Seven sika deer were introduced to Assateague in 1923.

*Sika* is the Japanese word for deer, though pronounced \'shē-kə\ in that language. *Sika deer*, then, translates to "deer deer." Smaller than white-tailed-deer, fawns and adults alike are patterned with white spots that provide camouflage in the dappled light of their forest habitats. Gracefully proportioned and lovely to behold, they are native to Japan, Korea, Siberia, China, Vietnam, and Taiwan. They are widespread as a feral species, with free-roaming populations in New Zealand, South Africa, Morocco, Australia, New Guinea, Great Britain, Ireland, Denmark, France, Austria, Switzerland, Poland, the Czech Republic, Russia, and parts of North America such as Texas. In 2006, the Assateague census counted roughly 400 sikas and 100 native white-tailed deer. Sikas can cause great damage to forest habitat. McCullough et al. (2009, p. 3), write, "no other deer can match the sika in its ability to strip the vegetation bare and expose soils to massive erosion—thereby creating a wasteland ... [the species has an] extraordinary capacity to negatively impact its own habitats." Unlike white-tailed deer, sikas are unlikely to confine themselves to home ranges. They move freely around the island and may also migrate seasonally, sometimes traveling up to 12 mi/19 km in a single 24-hr period.

The white-tailed-deer roaming the island are larger than sikas, but somewhat smaller in stature than their cousins on the mainland. In spring and summer, deer of both species are often bold, especially at dawn and dusk when they are the most active. During the hunting season, they become shy and sequester themselves in heavy brush.

Horses and deer have different dietary predilections. Deer tend to browse shrubs; horses do this infrequently. Sika and white-tailed deer tend to focus on devouring their favorite foods; horses consume a broader sampling of whatever is growing. Sikas eat bark from trees circumferentially, killing them; horses do not.

Assateague Island NS controls the sika and white-tailed deer populations through archery, shotgun, and muzzle-loader hunting seasons. Assateague is one of two public areas east of the Mississippi River where sikas can be hunted. Hunters remove about 130 sikas from the herd each year, keeping the population stable.

In January 2011, the sika hunt made national news when a hunter shot and killed a 28-year-old mare, which was found by another hunter some time later. It is assumed that the killing was accidental, but one wonders how an alert hunter could mistake a mature pony for a dwarf deer. The Park Service offered a $1,000 reward, and more than a year later, Justin B. Eason, 26, and his father, John A. Eason, 51, were convicted of the crime. The younger Eason, who shot the horse and left her to die, was ordered to pay $3,000 in fines and $2,000 in restitution for the horse and put on supervised probation for 18 months. The elder Eason was fined $1,000 and faced a year of probation for providing a false report, and both men were forbidden to hunt on federal lands for five years.

In the 1970s and early 1980s, the herd of 50–100 horses appeared to cause little damage to the Assateague ecosystem. Horse bands spread themselves widely over the island without overlapping of home ranges. As the herd passed 100 horses in the mid-1980s, horse grazing began to alter the tidal marsh environment. Growing bands of horses began to compete for resources where their ranges overlapped.

By 2000, the pony herd strained not only the island resources, but also the patience of Park officials. A larger herd led to more interaction between people and ponies. In 1975 only three young bachelors frequented the campground areas. Eight years later, 40 horses preferred to forage near the campsites. With more contact, more people were getting kicked and bitten, more private possessions were being damaged, and more horses were getting injured or killed on the road. Habituated to human doings, the ponies became bold and raided tents, screen houses, and garbage cans in search of food, scattering litter in the process.

The maintenance of a "desirable feral species" is allowed in certain circumstances under Park Service management policies as long it does not displace native wildlife. The horses of Assateague have cultural and economic value in that they are historically significant, people enjoy seeing them, and many visitors choose the park primarily to share their campsites with ponies.

One stated Park Service goal is to preserve a healthy herd of free-roaming horses that are subject to natural processes. Another goal is to protect key threatened species and island ecosystems, all of which are in jeopardy if habitat is overgrazed by voracious horses. Clearly it is important for the Park Service to control the equine population on the Maryland end of Assateague, but a balance must be struck between maintaining feral horses and protecting native and endangered species. How should one limit reproduction in a wild herd of horses?

The Chincoteague Volunteer Fire Company and the Fish and Wildlife Service limit equine population growth on the Chincoteague NWR by gathering the herd annually and selling most of the foals at auction. This roundup raises money for the Fire Company and keeps the herd population in balance. The Park Service was not interested in adopting a similar program for the Maryland herd, fearing that it would cause injury to horses and humans and increase the workload of an already overtasked staff.

By the early 1970s the U.S. Bureau of Land Management faced a similar problem in the herd management areas of the Western states and placed it in the hands of biologists Jay Kirkpatrick and

John Turner. Their solution was to develop a method of birth control for use on free-roaming horses. In 1988, with help from Irwin Liu of the University of California at Davis, they created a contraceptive that tricks a mare's immune system into attacking sperm as they try to penetrate the zona pellucida, the transparent, noncellular protein layer that surrounds all mammalian egg cells. Using the zona pellucida of pigs, they created an inexpensive, evidently harmless, and mostly reversible injection that essentially vaccinates wild mares against pregnancy without capture or restraint.

Since 1994, Assateague Island NS officials have maintained contraception through a yearly PZP booster, easily delivered by dart gun. At first, the seashore used the PZP vaccine to keep the herd's birth rate close to zero until it could decline from 166 horses to the target of 150. Foaling in 1995 in increased the population to 173, and decline proved much slower than expected. Even the scientists were surprised to find that contracepted mares live significantly longer than those allowed to reproduce at will. Mean age at death for untreated mares at the beginning of the program was just 6.5 years. By 2007, MAD for mares contracepted 3 or more consecutive years increased to 20. By 2013, the figure reached an astonishing 26+ years, comparable with the lifespan of a domestic horse. Treated mares not only lived longer, but also had a higher quality of life—their body-condition scores improved—and mortality for foals and other horses also dropped. Consequently, although the Assateague herd is no longer growing, it has taken a long time to shrink.

At first, the plan was to vaccinate all adolescent mares, then allow them to produce three foals each before halting their reproduction permanently. In 1998, the plan was revised to allow each mare to produce only two offspring, and in 2000, each mare was allowed to produce a single foal. Currently, fillies are vaccinated at puberty and contracepted for 3 years, after which vaccine is withheld until they foal. Once they have foaled, the vaccinations resume and they are contracepted indefinitely.

The equine population of Assateague has been extensively studied over recent decades, and the Park Service keeps records on the lineage and habits of each horse. This information allows biologists

to determine which horses to dart in order to prevent specific family lines from being lost from the gene pool.

Keiper's research suggested that minimal environmental damage would occur to the north end of Assateague if the pony population were kept below 150. Immunocontraception limited the growth of the herd, but by 2006 it became apparent to the Park Service that the 144 horses on the Maryland end were still disrupting the island eco-system. From 1994 to 2000, horses grazed upon saltmarsh cordgrass (*Spartina alterniflora) and* avoided saltgrass *(Distichlis spicata),* giving the latter a competitive advantage and changing the balance of each species in the marsh. Moreover, saltgrass cannot tolerate prolonged immersion in brackish water and does not trap and fil-ter sediment as *Spartina* does. The Park Service concluded that the horses were doing irreversible harm to the marshes of Assateague.

The agency recruited the Conservation Breeding Specialist Group to assess the free-roaming horse population and its hab-itat and evaluate how best to manage the herd. A diverse team of participants convened to discuss management objectives, past management plans, and the results of computerized population modeling. Its stated goal was to balance the desire for a large, healthy herd of horses with a healthy island ecosystem that favors endangered species.

An important consideration in any wildlife management project is effective population size, the number of individuals in a popu-lation that contribute offspring to the next generation. A healthy horse herd requires harems containing animals of reproductive age with enough genetic diversity to minimize inbreeding. A large population provides a diverse gene pool, but causes heavy damage to the ecosystem, which eventually harms the health of the horses themselves. A very small population would have more environmen-tal resources at its disposal, but inbreeding would eventually impair its health and render it vulnerable to disease and birth defects. Clearly, the optimal number of horses lies somewhere between the two extremes.

Effective population size is influenced by the fertility of indi-vidual animals, longevity, breeding cycles, sex ratio, mating strat-egy, and historic population size. Effective population size and census population size are not synonymous. A herd of 1,000 mares (none of which is pregnant) would have an effective population size of 0 because it is unable to pass its genes to a new generation without a stallion.

The definition of effective population differs with context and can have different mathematical and biological meanings, which are often confused or misunderstood. "Effective population size is a very complex term," says equine geneticist Gus Cothran (personal communication, April 20, 2011). "I have a book on my shelf with an equation for calculating it, and it takes about a page and a half. In a real population, the effective size is generally one quarter to one third of the census size. So that means that 150–200 individuals are required to have an effective size of 50."

Franklin (1980) proposed the 50/500 rule, derived from populations of fruit flies. According to this rule, populations with an effective population size less than 50 are at risk of inbreeding depression and extinction in the short term, and populations with an effective size of less than 500 risk extinction over the long term. The minimum population of 50 animals corresponds to rate of loss of genetic variability at 1% per generation, roughly half the maximum rate accepted by domestic animal breeders. Most conservation administrators recognize this "rule" as an overly generalized hypothesis that cannot guide management for species as different as snow leopards and salamanders.

The minimum viable population is an estimate of the smallest size at which a population can exist without facing extinction from natural disasters or loss of genetic variability. Conservationists usually consider MVP the number of individuals necessary to ensure 90–95% probability of survival of the group for 100 to 1,000 years.

This number, however, might not be sufficient if environmental catastrophe should wipe out a large number of animals. Drought, a brutal winter, or fire can quickly deplete a herd, as can disease. In the Assateague herd, between 1989 and 1993, at least 15 horses died of mosquito-borne eastern equine encephalitis, and 12 drowned in a single storm.

The concept of the MVP is useful, but implementation of any management plan involves reconciling scientific abstractions with environmental, political, financial, and logistical realities. Federal agencies, as a rule, consistently revise minimum numbers down. Regarding the Assateague herd, Zimmerman et al. (2006, p. 51) reported, "The PHVA participants recommended a short-term target population size of 80–100 horses, perhaps managing toward the lower end of this range." Conversely, horse advocates typically push for the largest sustainable population, arguing that

Optimum population size means different things to different researchers. Managers at Assateague Island National Seashore, using recommendations from experts in the field, determined that a population of
80–100 horses is the best compromise between environmental health
and the genetic and physical wellbeing of the herd.

lost genes cannot be restored, and outcrossing to increase variability may erode unique characteristics of the herd. Usually the
target population represents a compromise between the two fac-
tions. Says Cothran "In general, management agencies such as the
BLM or the NPS . . . want to keep the lowest numbers they can,
and so they go for the compromise numbers. For example, on the
Shackleford Banks, we figured that about 120 animals would be
acceptable, at least for a long time" (personal communication,
April 20, 2011).

To better analyze population dynamics, scientists create computer models that transform complex biological systems into simplified representations in hope of making accurate predictions. These models depict key features of the natural processes, but are easier to evaluate.

To explore the horse-ecosystem balance in the hypothetical realm, the Park Service used Vortex Population Viability Analysis software to simulate demographics, population trends, and environmental events. Data for each of the 56 stallions and 89 mares of Assateague gleaned from decades of research were fed into the software.

Vortex takes the horses through a "what if" scenario, inventing normal life-cycle events such as birth, death, and catastrophic events such as storms and disease. Every time the program is run, the result is different—horses have more offspring or fewer, horses drown in storms or do not, individuals are contracepted or are not. After the program had created 500 scenarios, participants gained insight into the probable outcomes of different management practices.

In creating these simulations, however, the Park Service assumed that the horses' reproduction is density-independent. But because horses are a K- selected species, equine herd growth is density-*dependent*. Since the creation of the national seashore, the herd has never been large enough to limit its own expansion.

Among zoo animals, when gene diversity falls below 90%, litter sizes become smaller, birth weights decrease, and young are less likely to survive. If the number of horses on Assateague exceeds 80 individuals, genetic diversity should remain above 90%, in the absence of natural disaster, and a visitor would probably see horses in the park on any given day. The Park maintains that a herd of 60 horses can remain more than 90% diverse if mares that carry the rarest bloodlines are allowed to bear most of the foals while the rest are strictly contracepted. A herd of 60 can also remain optimally diverse if two outside mares are added every 10 years.

Cothran disagrees. "Although 60 horses could retain 90% of the diversity, that is not a sustainable number in the long term," he said. An effective population of 50 is considered by conservation genetics people to be the lowest that could be sustainable, but effective size

is ⅓ to ⅕ census size, so we really are talking about a lot more than 60" (personal communication, September 10, 2014).

In the future, the Park Service may need to add horses to the Maryland herd if genetic variability declines or if disease or disaster threatens the population. The agency could choose these additions from other barrier island populations, such as Shackleford Banks, Currituck Banks, and Cumberland Island. The horses from these herds are genetically similar to the Assateague horses, yet different enough to revitalize the gene pool. They are also well adapted to life on a barrier island and so are likely to survive. Although the

The goal of population management is a healthy horse herd and a healthy environmental balance. This 2013 photograph seems to give evidence of a successful management plan. The horse, like the others the author observed that day, appeared in good flesh, and the marsh grasses remained dense and lush.

Chincoteague ponies originate from the same ancestral population, Cothran does not consider them good prospects for outcrossing. "They are so mixed genetically, I would not pick them unless the

A mare nurses her foal in front of the Assateague State Park administrative building. The immunocontraceptive program at Assateague Island National Seashore vaccinates mares against pregnancy to limit herd growth. Each mare is allowed to produce a single foal, then is contracepted for the rest of her life. Contracepted mares live an average of 9 years longer and remain in better health than mares allowed to reproduce naturally.

only objective was variability," he said (personal communication. September 10, 2014).

"Genetic diversity is currently good," says Allison Turner, biological science technician at Assateague NS (personal communication, February 17, 2011). "Barring a catastrophic event, additions should not be necessary in our lifetimes. Maintaining a genetically healthy viable population was a key consideration in determining the population size goal."

The Conservation Breeding Specialist Group final report in 2006 suggested a target population of 80–100 horses, maintaining the herd at the lower end of the range but adjusting the number upwards as needed. The Park service adopted their recommendations. Computer modeling suggested that under the 2006 management plan, the horse population would shrink to about 100 individuals by 2012,

80 by 2014, and 50 by 2016. By adjusting the rate of contraception, the Park Service might maintain the herd at a desirable level within this range or decreased further if necessary. A recent genetic study lowered the MVP threshold even further, concluding that the herd was genetically adequate with only 47 horses. Others argue that a herd of this size would eventually suffer the effects of inbreeding

A smaller horse population on Assateague means fewer conflicts between horses and visitors. To encourage people to keep their distance, the Park Service posted a Pony Patrol to follow bands, answer questions, and enforce the no-contact mandate. Caitlin Drummond, left, spent the summer of 2014 following Bayberry's band in the area of South Ocean Beach.

and would be more vulnerable to extinction through disease or disaster. Cothran comments, "I strongly disagree with the number of 47 being adequate. In 2–3 generations a serious decline in variation would be almost certain" (personal communication, September 10, 2014).

The Park Service hopes to offset the drawbacks of a smaller herd size by offering the visitor improved information and guidance on where to find the horses within the developed parts of the national seashore and Assateague State Park. It also intends to build an elevated observation platform to help visitors spot horses from a distance. The Park Service also plans to solicit community input through public meetings and online forums before making future management decisions.

Has maintaining fewer horses made a difference? Significant reduction in horse numbers is very recent, and research has yet to discover whether reduced grazing pressures have caused environmental improvements. Unofficially, however, park personnel point out benefits. "Historic data shows that beach-grass (*Ammophila spp.*) was the second favorite forage for horses, and horse grazing was significantly impacting dune formation and beachgrass proliferation," says Turner (personal communication, February 17, 2011). "We have noted reduction in those impacts recently."

Assateague and its horses are a "natural laboratory" and a valuable research resource. Many procedures used in the study of wildlife were perfected on the horses of Assateague Island, including remote pregnancy testing, fetal health evaluation, remote evaluation of endocrine function, immunocontraception, and fecal DNA analysis.

The Assateague horses are the best known and most loved of the wild herds of the Eastern Seaboard, and the closest to major cities and other dense populations. Over 2 million people visit Assateague's three parks every year, most of them remaining in the developed areas. Many come just to see the ponies. Attendance is heaviest from Memorial Day through Labor Day, peaking in July and August and reaching a nadir in January and February.

Visitors to the Maryland part of Assateague can readily see horses at roadside pulloffs, nature trails, and campgrounds, or they can hike out to find the more reclusive bands that keep to the wilderness areas. Despite heavy visitation, it is still easy to find empty beach and seclusion in nature if one is willing to walk a short distance. Free-roaming horses go about their business unmindful of human activity, and to watch them moving across the dunes in the heat of the day is to abandon oneself to a sense of affinity with the natural world. With thoughtful foresight, a balance can be achieved between horses, humans, and environment so that Assateague Island NS might be preserved in its natural state for the enjoyment of generations to come.

# References

Allen, A., Gill, S., Marcy, D., Honeycutt, M., Mills, J., Erickson, M., . . . Smith, D. (2010, September). *Technical considerations for use of geospatial data in sea level change mapping and assessment.* Silver Spring, MD: National Ocean Service.

Assateague Island National Seashore. (2006). *Feral horse management at Assateague Island National Seashore.* Retrieved from http://www.nps.gov/asis/upload/feralhorsemanag.pdf

Assateague

Associated Press. (1962, May 7). Former S&L head gets prison term. *Salisbury Times* (Salisbury, MD), *39*(122), p. 4.

Berger, J., & Cunningham, C. (1987). Influence of familiarity on frequency of inbreeding in wild horses. *Evolution, 41*(1), 229–231.

Boyd, L., & Keiper, R. (2005). Behavioural ecology of feral horses. In D.S. Mills & S.M. McDonnell (Eds.), *The domestic horse: The origins, development and management of its behaviour* (pp. 55–82). Cambridge, United Kingdom: Cambridge University Press.

Buchanan, M. (2003, December). *Horse manure management: A guide for Bay area horse keepers.* [Petaluma, CA: Council of Bay Area Resource Conservation Districts]. Retrieved from http://www.acrcd.org/Portals/0/Equine Fact

Center for Biological Diversity. (n.d.). *Seabeach amaranth.* Retrieved from https://www.biologicaldiversity.org/campaigns/esa_works/profile_pages/SeabeachAmaranth.html

Clean Water Act (Federal Water Pollution Control Act Amendments), 33 U.S.C. §§1251– 1387 (1972).

Coastal Waterbird Program. (2008, September 28). *Are there piping plovers nesting on your beach?* Lincoln, MA: Mass Audubon. Retrieved from http://www.massaudubon.org/PDF/cwp/piping_plover_landowners.pdf

Cohen, J.B., Erwin, R.M., French, J.B., Jr., Marion, J.L., & Meyers, J.M. (2010). *A review and synthesis of the scientific information related to the biology and management of species of special concern at Cape Hatteras National Seashore, North Carolina* (U.S. Geological Survey Open-File Report 2009–1262). Retrieved from http://pubs.usgs.gov/of/2009/1262/

Cothran, E.G. (2010, April 20). Personal communication.

Cothran, E.G. (2014, September 10). Personal communication.

De Stoppelaire, G.H., Brock, J., Lea, C., Duffy, M., & Krabill, W. (2001, July). *USGS, NPS, and NASA investigate horse-grazing impacts on Assateague Island dunes using airborne lidar surveys* (U.S. Geological Survey, Open-File Report 01-382). Retrieved from http://pubs.usgs.gov/of/2001/of01-382/

De Stoppelaire, G.H., Gillespie, T.W., Brock, J.C., & Tobin, G.A. (2004). Use of remote sensing techniques to determine the effects of grazing on vegetation cover and dune elevation at Assateague Island National Seashore: Impact of horses.

*Environmental Management, 34*(5), 642–649. doi: 10.1007/ s00267-004-0009-x

Diefenbach, D.R., & Christensen, S.A. (2009, August). *Movement and habitat use of sika and white-tailed deer on Assateague Island National Seashore, Maryland* (Technical Report NPS/ NER/NRTR—2009/140). Philadelphia, PA: National Park Service, Northeast Region.

Eggert, L., Powell, D., Ballou, J., Malo, A., Turner, A., Kumer, J., . . . Maldonado, J.E. (2010). Pedigrees and the study of the wild horse population of Assateague Island National Seashore. *Journal of Wildlife Management, 74*(5), 963–973. doi: 10.2193/2009-231

*Environmental assessment of alternatives for managing the feral horses of Assateague Island National Seashore: Finding of no significant impact.* (2009). Berlin, MD: U.S. National Park Service, Assateague Island National Seashore.

Feh, C. (1999). Alliances and reproductive success in Camargue stallions. *Animal Behaviour, 57*(3), 705–713. doi:10.1006/ anbe.1998.1009

Feh, C. (2005). Relationships and communication in socially natural horse herds. In D.S. Mills & S.M. McDonnell (Eds.), *The domestic horse: The origins, development and management of its behaviour* (pp. 83–109). Cambridge, United Kingdom: Cambridge University Press.

Franklin, I.R. (1980). Evolutionary change in small populations. In M.E. Soule & B.A. Wilcox (Eds.), *Conservation biology: An evolutionary-ecological perspective* (pp. 135–140). Sunderland, MA: Sinauer Associates.

Frydenborg, K. (2012). *The wild horse scientists.* Boston, MA: Houghton Mifflin Harcourt.

Gill, E. (1994). *Ponies in the wild.* London, United Kingdom: Whittet Books.

Goldschmidt, P.G., & Dahl, A.W. (1976, April). Estimating population in seasonal resort communities. *Growth and Change, 7*(2), 44–48. doi: 10.1111/j.1468-2257.1976.tb00305.x

Hayward, L. (2007). *State of the parks: Assateague Island National Seashore, a resource assessment.* Washington: National Parks Conservation Association.

Hinds, L. (2010, May 21). Personal communication.

Houpt, K. (2005). Maintenance behaviours. In D.S. Mills & S.M. McDonnell (Eds.), *The domestic horse: The origins, development and management of its behaviour* (pp. 94–109). Cambridge, United Kingdom: Cambridge University Press.

Houston, D., & Schreiner, E. (1995). Alien species in national parks: Drawing lines in space and time. *Conservation Biology, 9*(1), 204–209. doi: 10.1046/j.1523-1739.1995. 09010204.x

Ingle, M.C. (2005). *The development and testing of a procedure for monitoring visitor-horse interactions at Assateague Island National Seashore* (Unpublished master's thesis). North Carolina State University, Raleigh.

Keiper, R. (1985). *The Assateague ponies.* Atglen, PA: Schiffer Publishing.

Keiper, R. (2011, May 19). Personal communication.

Keiper, R.R., & Hunter, N.B. (1982). *Population characteristics, habitat utilization, and feeding habits of the feral ponies, sika deer, and white-tailed deer within Assateague Island National Seashore.* Research/Resources Management Report, MAR-4. Philadelphia, PA: National Park Service, Mid-Atlantic Region.

Kirkpatrick, J. (1994). *Into the wind: Wild horses of North America.* Minocqua, WI: Northword Press.

Kirkpatrick, J. (2014, May 29). Personal communication.

Kirkpatrick, J.F., & Turner, A. (2002). Reversibility of action and safety during pregnancy of immunizing against porcine zona pellucida in wild mares (*Equus caballus*). *Reproduction* (Suppl. 60), 197–202.

Kirkpatrick, J.F., & Turner, A. (2007). Immunocontraception and increased longevity in equids. *Zoo Biology, 25*, 237–244. doi: 10.1002/zoo.20109

Kirkpatrick, J.F., & Turner, A. (2003). Absence of effects from immunocontraception on seasonal birth patterns and foal survival among barrier island wild horses. *Journal of Applied Animal Welfare Science, 6*(4), 301–308.

Lambert, M.S., Ozbay, G., & Richards, G.P. (2009). Seawater and shellfish (*Geukensia demissa*) quality along the western coast of Assateague Island National Seashore, Maryland: An area impacted by feral horses and agricultural runoff. *Archives of*

*Environmental Contamination and Toxicology, 57*(2), 405–415. doi: 10.1007/s00244-008-9277-4

Levin, P., Ellis, J., Petrik, R., & Hay, M. (2002). Indirect effects of feral horses on estuarine communities. *Conservation Biology, 16*(5), 1364–1371. doi: 10.1046/j.1523-1739.2002.01167.x

Lowney, M., Schoenfeld, P., Haglan, W., & Witmer, G. (2005). Overview of impacts of feral and introduced ungulates on the environment in the eastern United States and Caribbean. In D.L. Nolte & K.A. Fagerstone (Eds.), *Proceedings of the 11th Wildlife Damage Management Conference* (pp. 64–81).

Mackintosh, B. (2003, October 27). *Assateague Island National Seashore: An administrative history*. Washington, DC: National Park Service, History Division. Retrieved from http://www.nps.gov/asis/parkmgmt/upload/asisadminhistory.pdf (Original work published 1982)

Maryland Department of Natural Resources, Resource Planning. (2005, October). *Assateague State Park land unit plan*. Retrieved from http://www.dnr.state.md.us/irc/docs/00011180.pdf

The Maryland Wetlands Act of 1970, Md. Env. Code Ann. §§ 16-101–16-503 (1970).

McCullough, D.R., Takatsuki, S., & Kaji, K. (Eds.). (2009). *Sika deer: Biology and management of native and introduced populations*. Tokyo, Japan, & New York, NY: Springer.

McDonnell, S.M. (2005). Sexual behaviour. In D.S. Mills & S.M. McDonnell (Eds.), *The domestic horse: The origins, development and management of its behaviour* (pp. 110–125). Cambridge, United Kingdom: Cambridge University Press.

McGreevy, P. (2004). *Equine behavior: A guide for veterinarians and equine scientists*. London: W.B. Saunders.

Monard, A.M., Duncan, P., & Boy, V. (1996). The proximate mechanisms of natal dispersal in female horses. *Behaviour, 133*(13/14), 1095–1124.

Naked rodeo on Assateague. (2007, August 24). *The Dispatch* (Ocean City, MD). Retrieved from http://www.mdcoast-dispatch.com/articles/2007/08/24/Cops-and-Courts/Naked-Rodeo-On-Assateague

National Environmental Policy Act of 1969, 42 U.S.C. § 4321 et seq. (1970).

Ocean City Planning and Zoning Commission. (2006, August). *Town of Ocean City Maryland comprehensive plan*. Ocean City, MD: Author.

Pendleton, E.A., Thieler, E.R., & Williams, S.J. (2004). *Coastal vulnerability assessment of Cumberland Island National Seashore (CUIS) to sea-level rise* (U.S. Geological Survey Open-File Report 2004-1196, Electronic Book). Retrieved from http://pubs.usgs.gov/of/2004/1196/ images/pdf/CUIS.pdf

Pilkey, O., Rice, T., & Neal, W. (2004). *How to read a North Carolina beach*. Chapel Hill: University of North Carolina Press.

Russo, B. (2009, October 30). Major sewer pipe project to disrupt OC highway. *The Dispatch* (Ocean City, MD). Retrieved from http://www.mdcoastdispatch.com/articles/2012/09/28/Top-Stories/Major-Sewer-Pipe-Project-To-Disrupt-OC-Highway

Rubenstein, D. (1982). Reproductive value and behavioral strategies: Coming of age in monkeys and horses. In P.P.G. Bateson & P.H. Klopfer (Eds.), *Perspectives in Ethology* (Vol. 5, Ontogeny, pp. 469–487). Princeton, NJ: Princeton University Press.

Rubenstein, D.I., & Hack, M. (1992). Horse signals: The sounds and scents of fury. *Evolutionary Ecology, 6*, 254–260.

Sanders, A.E. (2002). Additions to the Pleistocene mammal faunas of South Carolina, North Carolina, and Georgia. *Transactions of the American Philosophical Society, 92*, Part 5.

Seliskar, D.M. (2003). The response of *Ammophila breviligulata* and *Spartina patens* (Poaceae) to grazing by feral horses on a dynamic mid-Atlantic barrier island. *American Journal of Botany, 90*(7), 1038–1044.

Soper, S.J. (2012, February 24). Assateague horse shooter sentenced. *The Dispatch* (Ocean City, MD). Retrieved from http://www.mdcoastdispatch.com/articles/2012/02/24/Top-Stories/Assateague-Horse-Shooter-Sentenced

Sturm, M. (2007, May). *Assessment of the effects of feral horses, sika deer, and white-tailed deer on Assateague Island's forest and shrub habitats: Final report*. Berlin, MD: Assateague Island National Seashore. Retrieved from http://www.nps.gov/nero/science/FINAL/ASIS_horsedeer/ASISHorseDeerVegFinal_May07.pdf

Stuska, S. (2010, May 26). Personal communication.

Traill, L., Brook, B., Frankham, R., & Bradshaw, C. (2010). Pragmatic population viability targets in a rapidly changing world. *Biological Conservation, 143*(1), 28–34. doi:10.1016/j.biocon.2009.09.001

Turner, A. (2011, February 17). Personal communication.

U.S. Bureau of Land Management, Billings Field Office. (2001). *Environmental Assessment and Gather Plan, Pryor Mountain Wild Horse Range, FY2001 Wild Horse Gather and Selective Removal* (EA #MT-010-1-44). Billings, MT: Bureau of Land Management, Billings Field Office.

U.S. Bureau of Land Management, Elko District, Wells Field Office. (n.d.). *Proposed northeast Nevada wild horse eco-sanctuary.* Retrieved from http://www.blm.gov/pgdata/etc/medialib/blm/nv/field_offices/elko_field_office/information/nepa/eiss/archives/nenvwh_ecosanctuary.Par.21472.File.dat/EcoSanctuaryScopingBrief.pdf

Ward, R. (1998). Personal communication.

Weakley, A., Bucher, M., & Murdock, N. (1996). *Recovery plan for seabeach amaranth (*Amaranthus pumilus*) Rafinesque.* Atlanta, GA: U.S. Fish and Wildlife Service, Southeast Region.

Zervanos, S.M., & Keiper, R.R. (1979a). *Ecological impact and carrying capacity of feral ponies on Assateague Island National Seashore.* Final contract report to U.S. National Park Service, Mid-Atlantic Region, Philadelphia.

Zervanos, S.M., & Keiper, R.R. (1979b). Factors influencing home range, movement patterns, and habitat utilization in Assateague Island feral ponies. *Proceedings of Ecology and Behavior of Feral Equids Symposium* (pp. 3–14). Laramie: University of Wyoming.

Zervanos, S.M., & Keiper, R.R. (1979c). *Winter activity patterns and carrying capacities of Assateague Island feral ponies.* Report to U.S. National Park Service, Denver, CO.

Zimmerman, C. (1998). Personal communication.

Zimmerman, C., Sturm, M., Ballou, J., & Traylor-Holzer, K. (Eds.). (2006). *Horses of Assateague Island population and habitat viability assessment workshop: Final report.* Apple Valley, MN: IUCN/SSC Conservation Breeding Specialist Group.

# About the Author

Bonnie Urquhart Gruenberg is a multifaceted person who wishes that sleep were optional. She is the author of the award-winning textbook *Birth Emergency Skills Training* (Birth Guru/Birth Muse, 2008); *Essentials of Prehospital Maternity Care* (Prentice Hall, 2005); and *Hoofprints in the Sand: Wild Horses of the Atlantic Coast* (as Bonnie S. Urquhart; Eclipse, 2002), as well as articles in publications as dissimilar as *Equus* and the *American Journal of Nursing*. She is an artist and photographer and has illustrated all her own books.

By profession, she is a Certified Nurse-Midwife and Women's Health Nurse Practitioner who welcomes babies into the world at a freestanding birth center in Lancaster County, Pa. She obtained her MSN from the University of Pennsylvania after completing her BSN at Southern Vermont College, and she spent 10 years attending births in tertiary-care hospitals before returning to out-of-hospital practice. Prior to her career in obstetrics, she worked as an urban paramedic in Connecticut.

Horses have been her passion from infancy. For nearly two decades, she has spent countless hours researching and photographing the private lives of wild horses in both Western and Eastern habitats. She has been riding, training, teaching, and learning since her early teens, from rehabilitating hard-luck horses to wrangling trail rides in Vermont and Connecticut. In her vanishing spare time, she explores the hills and hollows of Lancaster County astride her horses Andante and Sonata.

More information and a collection of her photographs can be found at her Web site, www.BonnieGruenberg.com Additional information about the Atlantic Coast horse herds is on the Web at www.WildHorse Islands.com

Hoofprints Guide

If you liked this book, you may enjoy other titles by the author:

*The Wild Horse Dilemma: Conflicts and Controversies of the Atlantic Coast Herds* (Quagga Press, 2015)

The Hoofprints Guide Series (Quagga Press, 2015)
    Chincoteague
    Corolla
    Ocracoke
    Shackleford Banks
    Cumberland Island

Forthcoming

*Wild Horse Vacations: Where To See the East Coast Herds and What Else To Do While You're Visiting* (Quagga Press, 2015)

*Wild Horses! A Kids' Guide to the East Coast Herds* (Quagga Press, 2015)

Visit QuaggaPress.com for details.

43280483R00064

Made in the USA
Middletown, DE
05 May 2017